3RD EDITION

TEACHING & LEARNING MATERIALS & THE INTERNET

3RD EDITION

TEACHING & LEARNING MATERIALS & THE INTERNET

LEARNERS
MULTIMEDIA
COSTS
TEACHING
RESOURCES

IAN FORSYTH

KOGAN
PAGE

First published 1996
Second edition 1998
Third edition 2001

Kogan Page Limited
120 Pentonville Road
London N1 9JN
UK

Stylus Publishing Inc.
22883 Quicksilver Drive
Sterling, VA 20166–2012
USA

British Library Cataloguing in Publication Data

A CIP record for this book is available from the British Library.

ISBN 0 7494 3367 1

Typeset by Saxon Graphics Ltd, Derby
Printed and bound in Great Britain by Clays Ltd, St Ives plc

Contents

Preface

Disclaimer

In the initial 1996 edition of this book I wrote the following:

> This book is about educational and training course material being delivered using the Internet. It is not about the technical considerations of the Internet, although these are mentioned as needed. For example, it is not my purpose in writing this book to develop an argument for a particular platform, browser or any other operating system. If I were to do that, I would be offering a snapshot of the Internet as of today's date and some of what I would be writing would be out of date as I typed. The information you require for these technical specifications is best found on the Internet at the time you are ready to offer your course on the Internet.

In this 2001 version of the book I see no reason to change my stance. In the intervening five years, computing power has gone up and digital signal compression technology has the plain old telephone system (POTS) of copper cable (twisted pair) retaining a place in the distribution of education and training through a technological infrastructure alongside fibre optic cable, microwave and satellite technologies. What continues to be important is for the designers/developers of course materials wanting to deliver course materials via the Internet to focus on the educational requirements of a course and align this with the optimal use of the attributes of the technology and minimize the limitations imposed by technology. In this book the use of other technologies is discussed but the Internet is the focus. My underlying concern is that the 'hype' about the Internet has the potential to disguise its limitations as a tool for teaching and learning. These limitations, unless recognized, will result in an inappropriate use of the technology.

This inappropriate use will lead to failure or at least suspicion amongst learners and teachers. It will remind teachers and course developers of previous promises of technology to serve the purpose of education. Among more mature learners, in my part of the planet, these learners will be reminded of other technologies that failed to deliver.

As such, this disclaimer serves notice that this book about the Internet is dealing with the principles of content in a context and the infrastructure required to enable the potential of the Internet to service educational and training needs. Beyond that, it is recognized and supported that the Internet has the potential to serve the needs of the general community in their search for data to synthesize into information.

The intention of this book

The intention of this book is to examine the educational and administration considerations of offering a course or a selection of course materials for delivery via the Internet.

While the technical specifications of the capabilities of the Internet are changing over time, the need to consider course material and the appropriate means of handling that material on a delivery mechanism such as the Internet has several features that are relatively stable.

The considerations for putting educational material on the Internet are:

- Driven by an educational or training need to use the Internet as a delivery tool. This is discussed in Chapters 1 and 2.

- Educational and training questions raised by the possibility of informal access to data by a learner have been addressed. These are discussed in Chapter 3.

- That the contents of the course are not volatile in the short term; ie the 'calendar length' of the course offering. These and instructional design issues are discussed in Chapter 4.

Throughout the book the following possibilities are raised and reinforced:

- that it is possible for the learner to gain some sanctioning of learning or accreditation for informal learning, or gaining of data from the Internet, outside a procedural-based learning structure or within an institution providing sanctioned learning;

- that appropriate use of technology in relation to access by learners through the Internet and a consideration of the materials and learning strategies or processes have been addressed;

- that without due diligence the information rich will become richer, while the information starved… will starve.

Perhaps the last point is not an issue, if you are seduced by the notion of the Internet as a data superhighway…without a toll.

There are publications on the Internet and in hard copy about the use of the Internet. In most cases these focus on the possibility of achieving the Marshall McLuhan notion of the global village, or is it a village with global access to data? In my opinion, access to formal education and training on the Internet has a slightly different purpose.

In writing this book my intention is to focus on the formal educational and training possibilities available to educators and trainers through the use of the Internet as a means of delivery.

In previous editions of this book I admit that there is a question some will ask in that I have not used the Internet to publish this book. And therein is the explanation; this is a book, not an Internet document. It is a book about the educational use of the Internet. The technological features of the Internet are changing and will continue to change. The technology changes will enhance existing features of text, file transfer, chat and bulletin boards, graphics and illustrations, audio and video, modelling and virtual reality. These technology changes will need to be monitored to ensure that learners are not excluded from the learning process because of the technology. At the same time these technology options should not disguise the pedagogical strategies that exist. The pedagogy of using audio-visual features in other forms of delivery already exists. Because of this, it is possible to see how these features can be used for education and training for delivery using the Internet. It is possible to develop instructional design considerations, while the iterations of technology will only make these features more desirable, but questions about accessibility will need to be addressed.

If people want to join a discourse on the use of electronic communications, there are sites on the Internet.

Introduction

In this third edition it is still important to re-ask the question: What is the Internet and what is it becoming?

The simple answer is that the Internet is a conduit or electronic pipe (given the possibility of two-way communication, a road might be a better analogy). The Internet does not have an educational or training capability apart from linking educational and training providers to potential learners. This is written against a growing awareness that the free exchange of ideas that was at the genesis of the Internet is taking an increasing commercial focus. The growth of educational sites with a 'dot com' suffix rather than a 'dot edu' suffix is evidence of the need for commercial Internet companies to move into providing education as a source of revenue.

In many ways this is a new book because of the increasing commercialization of the Internet. However, many of the considerations in the previous editions still apply:

- appropriateness of the use of the Internet as a delivery tool of teaching and learning materials;

- issues of physical access and computing power;

- limitations to access because of socio-economic settings will arise with the advent of the Internet as a 'commercial' communications tool.

The current trends that are apparent on or related to the Internet are the commercialization of the Internet and the shift from the information society to information as a commodity.

These trends will have an effect on the changing paradigm of teaching and learning that is emerging in the use of the Internet as an interactive tool for education. This changing paradigm has been 'in the background' for decades in the form of new delivery technologies. The promise of many of these technologies has rarely been realized. The Internet has given the learner-centred paradigm of learning a reality. The reality is in eclectic learning.

Before exploring eclectic learning, the three prerequisite trends need a little discussion.

Trend 1 – Commercialization

At a conference recently, a speaker pointed out that the Internet-based company America On-Line (AOL) had a market capitalization exceeding those of Ford, General Motors and Boeing, combined! The growth of these electronic commerce (e-commerce) companies has been ballistic. However, there can be little growth without product and customers. The scramble in these e-commerce companies has been for clients and for product. Increasingly that product is information, or should that be data.

This leads to the second trend.

Trend 2 – From information society to information as a commodity

The Internet offers the potential for a person to access data to process into information in order to expand his or her knowledge (ie education). While this is a process that individuals go through in similar but different ways, the Internet holds the possibility for learners to satisfy their learning needs.

If the growth product for e-commerce is information, how are we to assign it value? Currently, information is assigned a value through the payment of commissions and royalty payments on sales to authors. It is not too difficult to find other examples of information equating to financial rewards. The sale of mailing lists or client contact lists will suffice.

The point to be made is that in many parts of the world Internet information is already a commodity and this has implications for the Internet as a delivery tool. The Internet has been seen as a 'free' source of information. Now providers are placing a business strategy over this information. This changes the promise of the Internet to support an information society into the Internet as provider of commodities.

There is already the emergence in the higher education sector of transnational and international consortia with the expressed aim of tapping into the international market for fee-paying students. In a similar but different activity, primary and secondary schools are taking an increasing presence on the Internet to promote the credibility of the school, attract more students and therefore more funding.

Trend 3 – The changing paradigm of teaching and learning

The impact of 'electric' technology on teaching and learning is not a new experience. In Australia the advent of the pedal wireless in the early 1930s for use by medical emergencies teams was immediately recognized by educators as a means of overcoming the vast distances of outback Australia in contacting students. The pedal wireless reduced the time of contact between teachers and students from weeks to a daily session on the 'School of the Air'. However, these interactive sessions were essentially teacher centred, and this has been the case with later technologies such as broadcast television, computer-based learning and the use of CD-ROM.

The availability of information over the Internet is changing the paradigm of teaching and learning. There are formal course offerings that mimic the paradigm of distance education. However, the emerging technological attributes of the Internet and the commercialization of information are the signal for a change in the paradigm of teaching and learning. At one extreme, the actual evidence on the Internet is the sites for term essays for students to download, rejig and submit as their own. The learners are in control. At the other extreme are the sites where satisfaction of course completion is negotiated to make sure that the learners' needs are met without quality compromise within the institution.

It is this shift in emphasis from the role of teaching to the learner that this book seeks to open up.

1 Using the Internet as a delivery tool for teaching and learning materials

Introduction

In the early days of Web browsers (eight years ago), the early designers of teaching and learning material for delivery on the Internet knew about the need for interactivity. There was also an obvious desire to show how smart they were because every whistle and bell that could be used, was used.

There still is a concern with users and some site developers of the social aspects of the Internet as a tool for education and training caused by this flagrant use of resources. In the near future, some of the concerns on access and interoperability will become part of the historical record. For the present, they remain real issues.

Today, considerations of 'instant gratification' that were beginning to rule the Internet or Web developer mentality are changing. Web developers are starting to realize that Internet users are wary of sites with long download times, or sites that require the download of 'special' applications so that indicated information eventually can be viewed on screen or as a printout.

The technology and the methodology to use the Internet as a tool for delivery of learning materials, or in a generic sense 'online learning', are evolving. During this evolution, it is possible to see two extremes in the use of the Internet as a delivery tool. Some educational institutions are putting course material online in order to be able to claim that they are a leading educational institution, because they have course material online. As a generalization, the course material is no more than an on-screen presentation of lecture notes. Fortunately, this seems to be a declining practice.

Other educational institutions have courses online showing every indication that online delivery factors have been considered. There are courses offered by educational institutions that fall between these extremes. It is understandable that educators see the delivering of course material online as desirable, particularly in the current climate of lifelong learning.

The use of flexible delivery methods is seen as the panacea for the continual upgrading of skills to cope with technological change. The use of the Internet as a delivery/interactive tool is the flavour of the month in flexible delivery.

The impact of technology on the paradigm of teaching and learning

It is becoming evident that there is a shift in the paradigm of teaching and learning as a consequence of the user/student ability to access information.

The shift in the paradigm is based in technology and under the control of learners. This learning process is enabled by technology and facilitated by industrial applications that minimize the need for bricks and mortar facilities like schools and universities. The new paradigm faces teachers with a fundamental challenge to their role and will ultimately cause that role to change. That the paradigm change is with us is evidenced not so much by examples (although these exist) but by the backlash that is evident in the attempts by teachers to control the technology that is the tool of the new paradigm.

However, the nature of the Internet technology seems to lead to confusion among the education and training fraternity. One view of the Internet is that it is a technology to deliver information. A more considered view is that access to the Internet as a technology and a delivery tool needs to be considered after the educational methodology is determined.

It is only through an analysis of the educational needs that the use of any technology or audio-visual device as a delivery tool is supportable. The requirements on the use of technology such as the Internet need to be on the factors relating to the course and effective delivery.

These factors are discussed below and relate to:

1 an analysis of the need for the course to be delivered via the Internet;

2 interaction between learners and teachers and the wider learning community: the conduit;

3 the ability of students to access the course information;

4 the resource implications for the educational organization;

5 maintaining the integrity of the course;

6 issues relating to administration of the course;

7 evaluation and reporting.

In this chapter and through the book, it is these factors that will be discussed.

The use of the Internet: a background

What is the appeal of Internet-based learning or network-based learning or online learning?

The appeal seems to be based on a belief that an information-rich society is developing. The developers at Microsoft, Netscape and other Internet providers seem keen to promote this position. What is generally omitted from the discussion are three considerations.

The first consideration is the need to place teaching and learning materials on the Internet, or is it access to educational materials via the Internet?

What is available via the Internet are formal courses and access to a vast amount of print, audio, video and computer-based learning materials. Each of these materials has pedagogical implications when it is used in a teaching space or accessed by learners. Therefore, what are the implications when these information sources are distributed, through the Internet, to a student's learning space?

The second consideration is the capability of learners to access this information. These include considerations of the learner's access and, given the eclectic data about courses and course content, the learner's meta-cognitive abilities.

The third consideration is the ability of learners to assimilate the information they find into their current knowledge.

And then there is the community of learning that might be associated with these offerings. This relates to the community of learning and the sanctioning of the learners' learning and that relates to the credibility of the Internet course.

I consider that the following factors are generic to establishing a site that has meaningful educational potential. The actual outcomes will depend on the data provided from the Web site, the degree of community of learning involved in the Web site, course maintenance, security, and the credibility of the Web site.

A traditional view of a community of learning involves the image of a group of teachers and learners. As a generalization, most people see learning as a process involving students and teachers. In a broader context, this activity is only possible when placed within a setting that involves administration of the institution and the students and staff. These considerations extend to all people who are stakeholders in education and training, and this extends into the wider community.

Within the setting of a community of learning, what are the factors that determine if a course should be offered via the Internet?

If the starting point is to determine the need of course delivery and the parameters that make the course offering educationally responsible and justifiable as an appropriate use of resources, I would like to emphasize that perhaps not all aspects or parts of a course are suitable for Internet delivery. In reality the need for Internet delivery should be based on the needs of the students and learning and the teaching infrastructure and the community of learning that this involves. The need for 'bricks and mortar' will remain as the paradigm shift evolves, and part of that evolution could well be the retention of 'bricks and mortar' settings as part of the social-ization process involved in education.

The seven factors for teaching and learning materials on the Internet are as follows.

1 An analysis of the need for the course to be delivered via the Internet

Why would you want to deliver your course or even parts of your course using the Internet?

Many educational institutions are putting courses on the Internet and are getting it wrong. In my opinion the main misuse of the Internet for course delivery is when printed, text-based material is translated into Web pages. This procedure is simplistic and denies the possibility of interacting with data offered by the Internet. These interactions have the potential to be as informing to the learner. That supposedly rational educational insti-tutions are doing this simple translation is a mystery.

If it is a mystery then some of that mystery needs to be exposed. A scan of journal articles on placing course materials on the Internet and a scan of courses currently available on the Internet suggest three possible reasons. The first is that by placing a course on the Internet there will be an increase in student enrolments. The second reason is that by offering the course on the Internet there will be cost benefits. The third reason is the belief by the institution (course organizer) that 'we can do better than them' (other institutions) in delivery of this course material through the use of the Internet. All of this denies that the Internet is just another technology tool for delivery of data.

Cave painting, clay tablets, papyrus, paper, film, audio recording, analogue video, digital video – each of these technologies when applied to education has its own pedagogical strengths and weaknesses. And then there is this thing called the Internet that is a means of distributing data and facilitating communication. As a tool of education, the Internet has no more credibility than face-to-face teaching, the use of distance education (postal) based technologies or satellite and computer online course materials. Where the Internet gains credibility in an education context is the capability to be interactive and resource rich. This is only matched by face-to-face teaching and learning and the use of the best of non-Internet computer-based learning where the focus is on the learner.

To co-relate these aspects of course delivery it is essential to see the Internet as a tool for delivery. The Internet is to be used when appropriate, using the electronic technology, using the strengths of the supporting technologies and minimizing the weaknesses of these technologies.

As we enter a period when the Internet is being seen as the technology to deliver course materials, it is essential to focus on the aspects of this technology that are educationally appropriate. The overwhelming attribute of the Internet is the capability of providing access to various sources of data and being a conduit for educational interaction to enable the learner to interact with peers and mentors as part of the learning process (see Figures 1.1 and 1.2).

2 The conduit

The Internet is a conduit. Rogers (1969) wrote that teachers are coordinators of learning experiences. This was the case for face-to-face teachers. In my opinion it is still the case for people developing courses for delivery via the Internet. Many of the considerations will be the same. These will include the need for backup material for the learners, question and answer options,

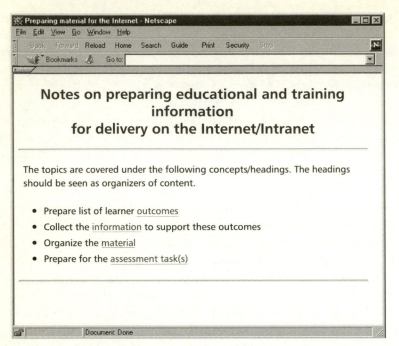

Figure 1.1   An Internet screen

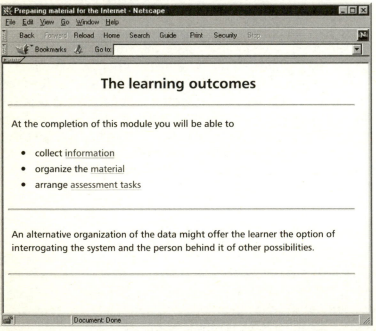

Figure 1.2   A statement of the learning outcomes for an Internet course

and the possibility for the student peer group to chat amongst themselves. The Internet becomes a conduit for coordinating learning experiences by learners, their peers, teachers as mentors and those in the educational community. However, the student must have physical access to the course and the ability and skills to access and utilize the course materials (see Figure 1.3).

Libraries, home, work, cybercafé and the new-generation mobile phones are potential access points to teaching and learning materials on the Internet. All of them come with some cost and this cost may limit access for some students. But that is in the world that I know.

Then consider this suggestion for the part of the world that I read about and see as images on television. Is it possible that aid agencies working in developing countries will need to hand out Internet devices and Internet connect time to support the agencies' work on the physical and nutritional needs of these people? By making available access to the data on the Internet they will ensure that these people, these countries, are able to overcome the poverty of information starvation and be participants in the global intellectual economy. Today, the intellectual economy goes hand in hand with the domestic economy.

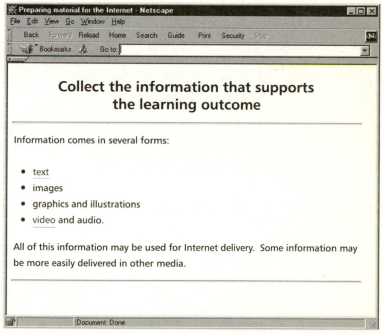

Figure 1.3 Navigation within core information

Then there is the issue of the students' ability to access and use the data educationally on the Internet.

3 The ability of students to access the course information

There is an assumption that students have an ability to use the Internet. This is based on observed behaviour. One of these observations is that male students are more likely to use the Internet than female students. This may be the case. But there are two means of accessing data. The first is by surfing the Web. This is an example of eclectic access to information. In other words, the student accesses Web-based data in a random manner and it is up to the student to assimilate that data into his or her current set of knowledge, skills and attitudes. This requires high-order cognitive skills and relates to meta-cognition. As a supposition, based only on the premise that females mature earlier than males, then perhaps they are more economical users of the Internet.

The second is by learners getting access to a set of data that is nested within an information set of boundaries. When students access such a Web-based course then, by design, there may be no eclectic capability in the site. In this case the student is forced to follow a predetermined pathway. This supports courses as topics rather than meta-learning.

However, it is possible to develop a Web course and have a degree of eclectic selection within the nested boundaries. This possibility relies on the use of scenarios. Scenarios serve to provide boundaries for the learner and the mentor/teacher to use the Internet (see Figure 1.4).

The issue of predetermined and eclectic pathways of learning represents the extremes of learning styles. It is suggested that no matter how the delivery of the material is designed, the issue of students being able to access the information in a manner that suits their learning style is critical.

4 The resource implications for the educational organization

Developing an appropriate set of course materials for Internet delivery need not have huge resource implications for the host institution. However, the institution, or the community of learning, needs to know what is proposed. Each department also needs to inform staff and students of course delivery changes. Then there are implications for staff training and development and the need for student training in new ways of learning.

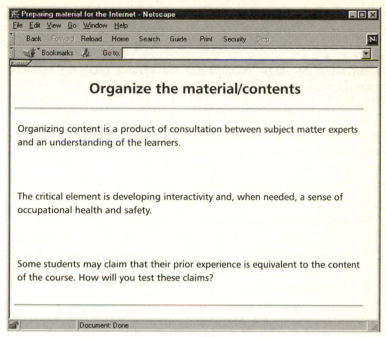

Figure 1.4   Considerations about organization

Given that the simplistic movement of pages of text on to an Internet site is not an option, then in my opinion the minimal resource requirements are a team consisting of a project manager, a subject expert and a technology-literate operator. This team could be augmented by a person with knowledge and experience in screen-based learning design.

The role of each is straightforward. The project manager has the role of maintaining the focus of the project. The subject expert provides the appropriate course content, while the technology-literate person translates the course content into a coherent delivery. The availability of a screen designer can affect the perception of the learner. This could be important for learner acceptance of the site.

Beyond this, the mandatory front-end analysis will determine the other resources or specialists required for development. These could be photographers, digitizers, text editors, etc.

Resources for delivery could include telephone support/helpdesk people, tutorial support and the considerations of tutor salaries, on-costs, and then there are the administrative staff involved in enrolment through to completion of the course process.

Having moved through this development phase, there is a need to have in place plans to maintain the course materials.

5 Maintaining the integrity of the course

Two main activities are required. The first is the team required to maintain the site. The second is the regime of updating the site.

In the best of worlds, an Internet course site needs to be maintained continually. This is different to responding to students' post mail, e-mail, sent-in requests and, as stated earlier, the instant gratification or response. This is part of the teaching–learning conduit.

To maintain the site you must have a technician and a subject matter expert. The technician maintains the site security while the subject matter expert maintains or in most cases monitors the site's educational credibility. With these two people a site could be maintained for a term/semester. The question then arises of long-term maintenance and this enters the realm of total course review or updating the site.

At some stage a course review will be identified. When this happens for Internet-delivered material there is a need to recognize that there are implications for enrolled and enrolling students. One consideration is how to handle students enrolled during a period of a course in transition. In the past, with course delivery or review it was time dependent. For students enrolled or enrolling in a course with Internet components, their contact with the Internet is time independent.

In the next section the long-term maintenance of the site is addressed and this is a question for administration.

6 Issues relating to administration of the course

In the previous sections, some of the issues relating to course content have been opened up. However, when it comes to issues of maintaining the credibility of the course, three aspects of administering the course are important.

The first concern is with security. This relates to the security of student information, the integrity of course material and the non-violation of assessment tasks. These concerns are related to the e-commerce aspects that Internet course delivery is moving towards.

With e-commerce a business has a product and it wants to maintain the integrity of that product and the relationship with its customer. With courses online we have the identical situation.

If an institution wants to offer a course online through the Internet then the people who buy course material expect confidentiality and security of personal information such as their PIN, accurate and up-to-date learning materials and access to support services. The students also expect confidential treatment of their assessment submissions and responses, including the grade levels they achieved.

However, I have a doubt about Internet security and the ability of any educational and training organization to have the resources to filter out viruses attacking e-mail systems, attacks on the information base of the course materials they offer and hacking into the administration of academic records. This last factor affects the use of the Internet as a part of the evaluation process.

7 Evaluation and reporting

When a student enrols in a course there is an expectation that some result will be recorded as an outcome: pass…fail. But what consideration is given to an evaluation of the course or the course materials?

Assessment of students in one form or another is part of any paradigm of education and training. Tests, essays and practicals cover the regime of actual tasks a learner may be called upon to undertake in order to demonstrate their expertise. But what evaluation is carried out on the course or course materials? What regime do course materials developers and deliverers put in place to determine if the Internet is more appropriate, effective or efficient as an educational and training delivery tool?

The questions that need to be resolved about the assessment of students include (see Figure 1.5):

- reporting to whom;
- for what purpose; and
- issues of reliability and confidentiality.

Reporting to whom?

An obvious expectation is that learners will require a report on any assessment they undertake. However, anecdotal reporting of non-completing, mature, distance-education students suggests that courses are undertaken and fees paid until learners have the information they require to support them in their business or for employment. In these cases the formal qualification is a secondary consideration.

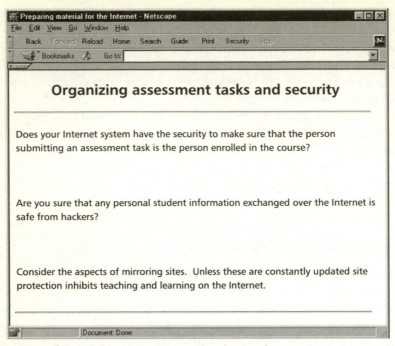

Figure 1.5 Organizing assessment and security

There are then the issues associated with reporting to employers who sponsor learners through a particular 'negotiated' course. What are the parameters for reporting to the employer that were set up during the initial negotiations for course delivery?

What are the reporting mechanisms that are agreed between the learner and the course deliverer at the time the learner signs on for the course?

Then there is the reporting that is either mandated or 'politically' responsible to the funding agents involved in the education process. This may well be government. It could also include parents, community groups, charitable organizations and sponsor or mentoring groups. The form of reporting to these members of the educational community will take different perspectives to 'satisfy' the accountability requirements of these funding agents.

For what purpose?

The essential purpose of the reporting process is to keep all the stakeholders informed.

As a consequence of an effective reporting process, the various audiences of learners, teachers, administrators, the community and the funding agencies are able to 'sign off' on an education and training process that is serving current needs.

A benefit of an effective reporting process is that it will alert the community of learning, the funding bodies and the various audiences of emerging trends in employment and lifestyles. This should enable the funding bodies and the educational community to accept shifts in funding priorities.

Issues of reliability and confidentiality

The education and training sector has a wide range of audiences. Reporting to these audiences includes the need for accountability and reliability of the information. There is a potential for conflict of interest to arise in this reporting process and between the various audiences that could lead to the confidentiality associated with learners' progression being compromised. An example of this is the 'performance table of schools' type publication of the performance of students in 'age-related' tests.

Confidentiality is also a question when learners' records are 'online'. At the outset, students are their potential worst enemies when it comes to confidentiality. The true 'urban myths' of learners swapping logon IDs and passwords are legion. With the proliferation of online courses and the (in)secure use of credit card over the Internet, the question for a course deliverer seeking an economic return is not so much one of who is doing the course but how many people have access to the Internet course material on the basis of a shared ID and password.

The question for the learner must be what is the effect on their academic/learning profile. For the eclectic learner this may not be an issue.

Conclusion

In this chapter a range of issues relating to the use of the Internet as a tool for delivery of course materials have been opened up.

These relate to:

- an analysis of the need for the course to be delivered via the Internet;
- interaction between learners and teachers and the wider learning community;

- the ability of students to access the course information;
- the resource implications for educational and training institutions;
- maintaining the integrity of the course;
- issues relating to administration of the course,
- evaluation and reporting.

The issues developed in this chapter form a backdrop for the considerations in the following chapters.

2 Interactivity, the five T's and the emerging paradigm

Interactivity

Interactivity is the critical factor in the use of the Internet and unless teachers are able to utilize this interactivity in their presentation of course material on the Internet, this Internet material will fail. The first reason for failure is that there is a lack of the five T's. The second is that the real revolution has to do with content, context and the ownership of information that is now available to the learner: this is the paradigm shift.

The five T's as a problem

There are four T's for teachers' lack of use of technology in the paradigm of teaching and learning, and the reasons that control of learning will pass from their hands are as follows. The fifth T has to do with the infrastructure issues that are in any innovation process. And the use of the Internet is an innovation process that is evolving.

The T's are as follows.

T1: time

The use of technology to deliver education and training requires a different timeframe for development of the courses and materials and a different notion of the use of time for those using technology in education and training.

Technology changes the role of the user and therefore the time that the lecturer, teacher or trainer devotes to tasks. It is certain that one cannot embrace technology without heavily modifying one's perceptions of the traditional uses of time. In this aspect alone the use of technology demands that teachers reconsider how they 'spend' their time. Many teachers seem reluctant to alter their time allocation and as a consequence shun technological innovation. This failure to adjust could be caused by one of two reasons:

1   Teachers hoped that technology would 'go away', and there are examples in the past of teaching innovations that have not lived up to claims.

2   Although they may control the curriculum, teachers failed to recognize that they no longer control the data. Teachers who spend all their time defending the curriculum are expending an amount of energy that is misplaced. The defence of the curriculum is at the expense of losing control of the teacher's real skills in support of learners through support, mentoring, information distribution or the ability to challenge learners on their information, skills and abilities.

T2: technology timid

The use of technology to support learning requires expertise and the gaining of this expertise is seen as daunting by many teachers. This should not be the case. The expertise that is required to use the technology is that of education and training for the appropriate use of technology in the learning context.

This familiarity with the technology makes technology transparent and the subject matter, the realm of the teacher as expert, is given its prominence. Inappropriate use of technology makes the technology the focus of the activity, not the knowledge, skills or sensitivities that should be the focus of the learner's attention. It is only through appropriate use of technology that reluctance to use technology is dispelled, because appropriateness gives relevance. And the determiners of what is relevant in terms of content should be teachers and learners. However, it is learners who will use the technology to access the information they require when teachers ignore technological means of optimizing access to data and the potential to learn. This access by students will be by the most efficient, accessible and most innovative means available to them.

As a saving grace for teachers, some learners may determine that the human database of a teacher is one appropriate reference point.

T3: territoriality on topics

Just as the appropriate use of technology makes the technology transparent, technology demands that the artificial barriers erected around topics be torn down, or at least made negotiable. Topics don't exist in isolation and the web of concepts that form the corpus of any subject needs to be exposed. More importantly, the artificial barriers are not maintainable with the new technologies and the ability to access various information sources is not controlled by the tyranny of teachers or curricula. The clarifying question is not so much 'What do you need to know before you learn this?', but 'What do you know and what knowledge, skills and attitudes do you want to build in the foreseeable future?'

T4: training

In the traditional education paradigm, training to use new technology was tried. Perhaps in hindsight the wrong people were trained. Training tended to focus on the teachers. Training for the learner was only permitted within the parameters comprehended by the teacher. Any extension outside these parameters was seen as a threat to the role of the teacher as expert and to be avoided.

The new paradigm requires training of the learner. However, this training must not be at the mechanistic level that is exemplified by most training on how to use a computer and seems designed to increase the level of mystification about computers. No such mystification exists about a car or the telephone but both in their own ways are complex mixtures of parts, wires and 'bits'. Yet to most lay-people, so long as the car or telephone works that is good enough. However, people still need to be trained to use a car or a telephone with effect. Therefore the training needs of people need to be addressed from the point of view of functional utility rather than formidable complexity. This training for new technologies must focus on the new paradigm appropriate to the technology, not 'force-fitting' the technology to content or content to technology. If this training is not available, the learners will train themselves. This has happened in the past when people 'educated' themselves. This is precisely what computer-hackers do.

Computer-hackers train themselves and network with others to access data. The mere fact that the economic and military establishment declares this illegal does nothing to dismiss the point. The learning activity of hackers is purposeful eclectic education. Hackers seek the data they want from sources available and appropriate to their needs. As Rheingold (1992) states, '[Hackers are seen as] anti-social urchins who break into other people's computers. Originally the term was a more honorable reference to the virtuosity of some programmers in finding ingenious ways to overcome obstacles. Indeed without hackers we wouldn't have personal computers or public computer networks today' (Rheingold, 1992: 178). The hacker and the eclectic learner have taken on the mantle of finding ingenious ways of overcoming 'learning' obstacles.

T5: truss – an infrastructure requirement

During the construction of a building you frequently need to create a structure or support to help the building do its job. There may need to be a span over an open space, or the need to provide a cantilever. To help during this stage of construction you put in a truss or a support. Frequently, in introducing or developing educational and training initiatives we forget the need for support. And for want of that support the educational construct falls into ruin. This lack of support is seen in the field of innovation in education.

However, this need for a truss to support learners and to facilitate learning does not lie solely within education. For education to remain relevant, the people involved in the process must do a 'reality check' within the wider educational community. That this check rarely seems to be done at all leads to a second set of reasons for the lack of technology in the paradigm of teaching and learning.

Margret Bell (1993) lists eight reasons for the failure of information technology (IT) to have an impact in schools:

- no coordinated vision

- little or no evidence of what works

- information is inadequate and is limited

- IT in learning is not always related to solutions of real problems

- senior managers are not taking a strategic management of change approach

- educators lack confidence and competence in use of IT

- insufficient or inappropriate equipment

- insufficient or inappropriate software

   (Bell, 1993: 7)

Whilst many of the problems Bell outlines relate to failure of innovation, her assertion that educators lack confidence and competence is further support for the argument to move the focus of technology away from teachers to learners. The emerging paradigm changes the central function of the teacher in terms of context and content in education and training. The new paradigm by its very nature bypasses teachers attempts to construct pathways to understanding, behavioural objectives, negotiations and empowering the learner. The new paradigm is the learner, with the tools of technology, involved in eclectic education.

The emerging paradigm

The characteristics of the emerging paradigm are summed up as follows. The information and education and training to be had are in the public domain, access to this material is public and eclectic, with the organization and verification of outcomes taking place in public. This is based on the technology being controlled by the learners and is a reflection of the access possible in the information age. The possibility exists for learners to develop their expertise through their activities, with their meta-learning assisted by technology.

This eclectic learning should not be seen as learning at random. The learning appears to be inconsistent, but then when you compare learners in a classroom, the learning is not a consistent progression. If it is not so, a great deal of energy is expended on ensuring (read insuring, or demonstrating to the taxpayer through national-based skills tests) that the intended outcomes are achieved.

Eclectic education supports meta-cognition and meta-learning. Schmitt and Newby (1986) developed a diagram to explain meta-cognition. They reason that meta-cognition is predetermined by knowledge and regulation (Figure 2.1).

While Schmitt and Newby include the precondition of an understanding of personal cognitive resources and task requirement, a more

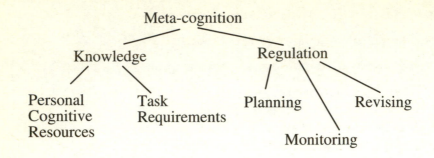

Figure 2.1 Explaining meta-cognition

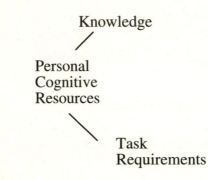

Figure 2.2 Altering the knowledge side

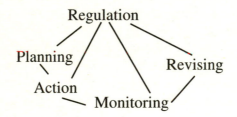

Figure 2.3 The regulation side

realistic relationship would be that it is through personal cognitive resources that the requirements of the task are comprehended. This would alter the knowledge side of the diagram (Figure 2.2).

Schmitt and Newby incorporate activities of planning, monitoring and revising in the regulation aspects of meta-cognition. However, without

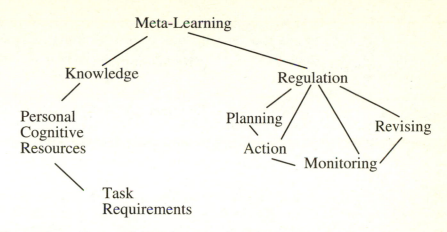

Figure 2.4   Preconditions for meta-learning

action, the regulation process lacks motive to monitor and revise. Without action there is no need for further planning. As such, the regulation side of their diagram would be better represented as in Figure 2.3.

In the same manner the preconditions for meta-learning include knowledge about learning and how this is applied to the task. Again, knowledge about learning strategies will affect the way in which a task is perceived, while regulating the learning will require planning, action, monitoring and revising (Figure 2.4).

The development of these skills is required for eclectic education and support aspects of on-the-job and just-in-time learning. The more traditional paradigm of education, with the focus on the teacher, does not encourage autonomy of action and independence, that is, meta-cognition and meta-learning. Meta-cognition and meta-learning are in stark contrast to the classroom model, without denying that the classroom is a suitable venue for certain educational and training activities, as is the Internet.

As an aside, the assumptions about individuals' place in their organization (on the left of the diagram) and the similarity to a quality circle (on the right of the diagram) are not a pure coincidence with the proposition of eclectic education as a positive outcome-driven activity of the learner.

The eclectic/generic approach to Internet course delivery

This approach requires an adoption of the implications in education and training reform, open and flexible delivery, just-in-time education and training and work-related learning. In these settings the need for a formal course may not be required. What may be needed is a set of materials to satisfy a need for a small number of competencies to be addressed, drawn from different subjects.

Example

A company or an individual (note: not an industry) might need to retrain staff/upgrade their skills owing to a technological change within the company. In this situation they will require a course suited to their needs, not a course based on industry norms. While an industry-based course, in the long term, might satisfy the need, it may not address the immediate knowledge and skill requirement. The response of the education or training provider should address the immediate need and this could be through an eclectic or generic approach.

The eclectic/generic approach would have the learner or client company, the subject expert and an instructional designer look at the learner or company educational or training need and develop a plan of action. This would have the learner or the client organization involved in a process of identifying their requirements. The education and training organization is then in a position to evaluate the learner/client needs in terms of support material so the expected outcomes will be achieved. At the same time, the learner or company becomes an active learner. They have become an active part of the learning process through:

- their involvement in defining the need;
- taking part in the analysis of content and appropriate delivery strategies to account for the learners;
- establishing means of verification of learning; and
- being part of the evaluation process to verify that needs have been met.

In this scenario the Internet is a tool for delivery of all or part of the agreed education and training. The Internet may still be an initial contact point in the above scenario but it becomes a means of communication about education and training, not a repository of established courses. There are, however, the possibilities of some generic educational and training materials such as Occupational Health and Safety. These materials could exist in a generic form to be 'fine-tuned' for the specific requirements of eclectic requests for materials ranging from childcare to spray painting (see Figure 2.5).

Conclusion

This chapter set out to be a point of departure, to enable you to start thinking about the underlying or deeper considerations for creating meaning in the development of a course for delivery on the Internet. I cannot make the point too strongly that the ultimate success or failure will link back to the effort put in at this analysis and planning stage.

In the next chapter, and on the basis of the change in the teaching and learning paradigm, the focus is on the learner. The potential of consortia as a means of financing the Internet delivery of course material and the use of scenarios as a means of grounding Internet material within the learners' prior experience are discussed.

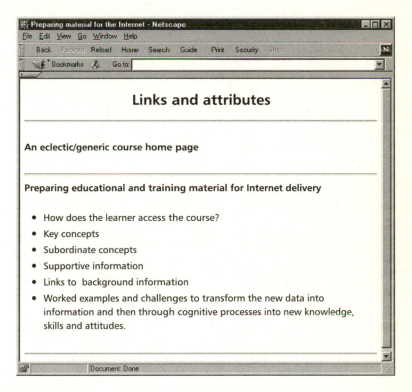

Figure 2.5 An eclectic/generic course home page

3 From learner focus to scenarios to consortia

Summary

Within this book the notion of a paradigm shift in education and training is proposed. The shift is in the emphasis from teacher as focus or controller of learning processes and strategies to satisfying the needs of the learner. This is supported by considerations of structuring information to support meta-cognition in the process of meta-learning.

On a practical level the question becomes one of how do teachers and learners accommodate the learning possibilities of learning content from the Internet that may be suitable for eclectic learners and could satisfy the more structured approach to learning of the traditional course providers. One option to cover the spread of learner competencies and the need to offer course material in the current expectation of 'surfing the net' is the concept of scenarios.

As a support mechanism for the development of scenarios, the need to develop consortia is proposed as a means of optimizing options and minimizing costs.

Genre/scenarios

In preparing an earlier edition of this book I tried to be conservative in approach, yet it is apparent that developments on the Internet are moving rapidly. For example, any discussion on the use of virtual reality would have been considered by most to be a discussion for the future, yet VR already 'exists' on the Internet. In the same manner, the future that is already here is the discussion of genres or scenarios that have been introduced in this edition.

In my opinion, the consideration of genre as a means of organizing material is a two-edged sword. Most people are happy with a discussion of genre as it relates to works of fiction. The construct of a love story involving 'boy' and 'girl' generally follows the pattern of they meet, they fall apart or are separated and then are reunited. The adventure story sets out to have the main characters achieve a goal. Like the love story, the ultimate goal is happiness. The detective story also has characteristics, which might include a *femme fatale*, a red herring (false trail) and a confrontation with the villain. The point of discussing fiction genres here is to point out that the narratives developed in any of these genres generally follow a pattern. The settings in which these patterns emerge can range from the past to the future. So it is possible to have a murder mystery set in the 12th century involving poison and a murder to be solved by Sherlock Holmes in the later years of the 19th century or some robotic sleuth of the 22nd century.

If we consider the activities in an educational setting, then it is arguable that most teaching and learning activities could be classified as having genre characteristics. At a simplistic level, instructional events fall into three categories. These are tell, show and do. This rather simple troika covers a range of activities from simple to complex, and interplay between the three. For example, in the face-to-face setting of education and training the use of tell, show and do could fluctuate not just as a result of the teacher's plan for the lesson but as the teacher responds to clues for further telling, showing or doing, which are generated by learner responses. Those of you with memories of teacher training, or current experience in competency-based teaching, will have the regime of objective to be taught, competency to be demonstrated, and the activities, resources and assessment events to be used and worked through by the learner.

As a generalization, these are teaching events. What are the learning events that the teaching events are expected to trigger? The learning events 'must' trigger attention, 'must' lead to assimilation of the new information, 'must' lead to trialling by the learner of the new information to generate comprehension, 'must' lead to demonstration of new 'understandings' as a result of the teaching. However, the terms tell, show and do are too simplistic because they do not recognize the ask, respond and verify actions undertaken by an increasing group of independent learners.

In this setting it is possible to see the development or (more correctly) the potential to make obvious the genres or scenarios that exist in education and training. Most learners will have experience of the tell, show and do and even the ask, respond and verify types of actions. From a learner's point of view (though not their vocabulary), these could be considered as didactic, vicarious and practical learning events. Each of these expressions reinforces a view of teaching as tell, show and do. The expressions also open up ways in which learners are able to access material.

Didactic, vicarious and practical genres or scenarios are a scheme to make rational the process of translation from course document to teaching and learning activities for the Internet:

- Didactic instructional events are those where the learner expects to be provided with information. It is also an expectation that the learner will at some later stage use that information beyond a responding interaction with the teacher. However, a didactic event could be triggered by a learner's inquiry.

- Vicarious instructional events are those where the learner is an observer. It is an expectation that the learner will at some stage demonstrate that the observation has been assimilated into their knowledge, skills and attitudes.

- Practical instructional events are those where the learner is a participant trialling and demonstrating expertise.

In teaching it is a truism to claim that the translation of the initial course documentation to the actual teaching situation goes through several stages. However, there seems to be a lack of sophistication at the crucial stage of translation from the course documentation to the material that is eventually delivered to learners. One consequence of this is that stereotypical teaching and learning activities are developed. These activities are seen as being economical for teachers to develop. The ability to recycle or force-fit activities tried in the past is possibly a saving in time for the teacher and costs for the institution. However, these stereotypical responses may not address the challenges to learners required by skills upgrading courses and the requirement for lifelong learning.

If the Internet is to be used to assist teachers and learners to move away from the stereotypical reaction in the translation of course documents to teaching materials and activities, certain processes and assumptions need to be challenged. These include the assumption that course documents are developed around appropriate competencies. While it is true that competencies in many areas are stable, there are areas such as information technology, and the areas that information technology impacts on, where constant change is the norm. In these areas the ability to develop course materials will depend to a large degree on the skills and abilities of the teachers to keep pace with change. Yet in many institutions there is an expectation that the process of translating the content into teaching and learning activities is precise.

In reality, there is a lack of precision caused by handing the course documentation to those who will deliver the material in the expectation that all practitioners have an equal understanding of the implications contained in the documentation. In many industrial process-based situations, such as the appropriate use of machinery, or the need to train operators in the methodology of obtaining valid results from sample testing, a lock-step approach is required. However, there are other areas within courses where a lock-step methodology could be a limitation for the learner. If for example, there is the need to comprehend the implications of a variety of indicators during a process, a lock-step methodology may not be appropriate. The learner will be expected to search through a 'catalogue' of possibilities and determine a 'best course of action'. These types of activities require the learner to have experience of or information about a wide range of possibilities. The limitation is that the education and training is seen as subject specific and the skills involved are not seen as 'transferable'. This limitation could result in restricted employment opportunities in the future.

There is a further limitation when the lock-step approach is used for courses offered as retraining, or for upgrading skills for more mature people. Mature learners already have skills and knowledge and become frustrated if they are forced to theorize or practise knowledge and skills already gained. In this situation the institution loses credibility. However, the learners stay in the course to gain their qualification, but will be reluctant to recommend the course to others. Therefore enrolments fall. With falling enrolments the course is no longer viable and it should be taught no more…?

The challenge is to keep courses viable by being appropriate to the needs of the economy and/or society. This challenge of translation of course documents into courses and keeping courses relevant seems to be predicated on a notion that having developed a course it is then a matter of selection of teaching strategies and resources. It is as though on one hand there are courses and on the other hand there are teaching strategies and resources and it is a simple matter of bringing the two hands together.

The scenario

A scenario provides the learner with a context in which course materials are presented and course outcomes are a stated expectation. The use of a scenario in an educational and training context is aimed at placing the learner in a holistic learning environment. Diagrammatically it can be represented as shown in Figure 3.1.

This figure represents the potential of scenarios to connect the principles and practicalities of a course within the wider context, enabling learners to bring whatever experience they have to the learning tasks. The figure has an inference of a linear progression. There is an indication that there is an overlap within scenario 2. What is more important in the consideration of learning in an eclectic environment, such as the Internet, is the position of

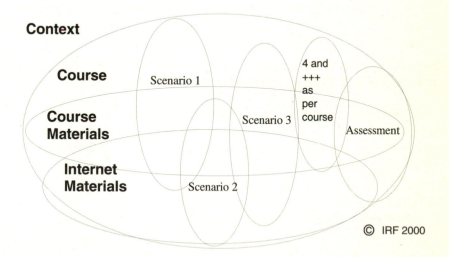

Figure 3.1 Scenarios in relationship to course, course materials, the context and assessment/outcomes

assessment. Diagrammatically the positioning of the assessment task is an attempt to represent that the outcome is more part of the ability to work in the context. This is a traditional view for education and training and for employment. In many cases of education and training, the same figure could be seen as shown in Figure 3.2.

In this case the learner is asking what they need to demonstrate to pass the course. This can be covered by Recognition of Prior Learning (RPL) and further study. This is an appropriate scheme for sanctioning learners of all ages.

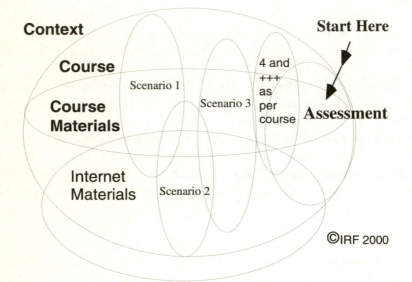

Figure 3.2   A more probable path for a 'mature' learner in assessing their use of an Internet-delivered course

However, it is possible that neither of the scenarios shown in Figures 3.1 and 3.2 fits some context/course/course materials. Therefore scenarios are not being presented as a panacea. The following chart indicates the strengths and weaknesses of the use of scenarios on the Internet:

Strengths	*Weaknesses*
Provides context	May be too case specific
Limits globalization of response	Limits global response
May be generic across an industry or subject area	Generic setting may not work with further customization
Enables work within a broadly defined area	May pinpoint specific strengths and weaknesses in the learner

A concluding point about scenarios

Scenarios must be developed in a context that:

- reflects a version of the 'real' world;

- suggests options to explore possibilities within this 'world';

- ensures that the skills of the learner are reflected in a response by the learner showing competencies and knowledge.

The development of scenarios leads again to the consideration of the resources available to Web-site development within an organization.

Consortia: schools, colleges, universities and Mammon

During the 1990s, if you wanted to win a research grant the 'trick' was to form a consortium. Inter-university and industry groups pooled their skills in support of claims for research funds. For the funding bodies the development of such consortia had the merit of optimizing the use of limited funds, promoting the need for collegiate action and reducing duplication. It was also cheaper!

In the post-compulsory education sector similar moves towards course development and delivery using the Internet are emerging. These developments include transnational as well as national consortia. University 21 is one initiative, while the MIT and the University of Cambridge are reported to be in discussion on a consortium-like undertaking. (When you read this… Has it happened? Or has the edu.dot been replaced by a dot.com?)

At the school level, community and state-based or regional-based curricula should retain a place. However, in certain instances a more contextualized view of the content needs to be available to learners. This is a context that enables learners to start to, or continue to, develop their meta-learning skills. It is through a consortium style of arrangement that a wider world-view is possible. At a simplistic level, for school students it is 'pen-pals on the Internet' with the buzz of almost instant gratification that even airmail cannot provide.

Course offering through the development of consortia has the potential of developing economies of scale beyond those available to a single institution. And they are the result of no single institute having sole rights to any branch of knowledge. These economies will be both in development and in delivery.

The biggest drawback in forming a consortium is the negotiations. Against a background of rivalry between institutions, between faculties within an institution, between people working in the same field of education and training, the potential to form a consortium with a wider perspective would have seemed doomed. The Internet has the potential to change this. In the current form of the Internet, free exchange of ideas and dialogue is encouraged.

While hoping that the Internet will encourage consortia, I do hold fears that the commercialization of the Internet will alter its availability as a 'free access option' and therefore education and training options to learners.

In developing a consortium there are two rationales. Both are based on the perceived and hopefully agreed outcomes of the enterprise. In both cases resourcing will be an issue.

The development of a formal consortium has a diagrammatic presentation shown in Figure 3.3. The diagram is based on an agreed long-term association, over different projects of mutual benefit to all parties. The figure represents an ongoing relationship between the parties.

It is possible to form a more informal consortium. This is best represented in the education and training needs within a company, rather than an industry. The consortium is formed for a single-purpose activity, for a

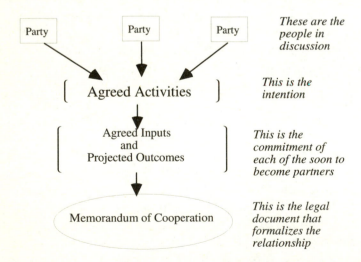

Figure 3.3   Formalizing a consortium (© IRF 2000)

defined period and for a specific outcome. The informal consortium has the aspects shown in Figure 3.4.

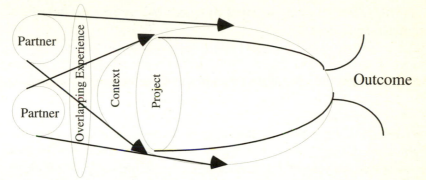

Figure 3.4 An informal consortium education and training arrangement within a context (© IRF 2000)

As a comparison, the following strengths, weaknesses, opportunities and threats (SWOT) chart sets out the position on consortia:

Strengths

Spreads the load in development, production and delivery

Aggregates expertise in subject matter, instructional design and delivery and evaluation of the learners and the effectiveness of the course

Has global potential

Focus the expenditure of energy and money

Are a preferred model for funding bodies

Are vibrant and seek new collaborators

Weaknesses

Latent rivalry at institutional or interpersonal levels

Depends on the commitment of individuals

Can dissipate energy

Can become moribund and inward looking, self replicating

Set up with enthusiasm but little support infrastructure of capability

Lock out external views and therefore lose context

Opportunities

Draw on expertise not available within a single institution

Provide course material for students not possible within the resources of a single institution

How well partners are supported within their own institution

Threats

Exposure to partners who do not conform

If you do not…then others will and you will be locked out

A final point for the consideration of consortia and learners must be taken into account. This point requires an examination of the value added for learners should they choose to work through an educational consortium. The consortium may offer a feel of being 'global' but it must not forget that its offering is local.

Summary

The Internet is a communication tool and there is a growing awareness in the education sector that the Internet is a means of gaining added student enrolment dollars. However, accessing these courses on the Internet provides evidence of duplication of course offering, leading to the inevitable conclusion that there would be confusion for the students about the most appropriate course in which to enrol, a frustration with the education community because of this multiple course offering, the technology and resulting in a real waste of resources.

4 Getting started: the Internet and instructional design

Summary

There is little experience in using the Internet as a teaching and learning tool. There is experience and research on computer-based learning. This has given insights to elements of screen design, the development of interaction through online and off-line working, file transfers and the evolution of the computer into an audio-visual communication device. It is my hope that through the examination of a SWOT analysis of the Internet and the problems of computer-based learning, when courses are made available through the Internet there will be effective teaching and learning in the material.

At the moment there is very little experience of delivering courses via the Internet. However, there is a field of experience in delivering courses by computer and one expectation is that the same strengths and weaknesses that apply to computer-based learning will apply to some aspects of teaching and learning on the Internet.

However, these are not the only considerations. Currently there are available computer-based tools that allow the direct conversion of a word-processed file to pages on the Internet. These are HyperText Mark-up Language (HTML) and Standard Generalized Mark-up Language (SGML).

There is Hot Java for graphics, Page Mill and Site Mill for page and site maintenance and a virtual reality modelling language alongside a version of CAD that provides 3D modelling. As I write this, Microsoft Word has an add-on called Internet Assist. By simply (it is almost simple) converting the file from a text (.doc) file through the use of a 'save as' process a standard word-processed document is converted into a scrollable HTML text page that could be used on the Internet. I write 'could be used' because all that happens is a simple conversion. In my opinion more than just a simple conversion is needed to make text material suitable for use on the Internet. If this is the cheap and easy way you want to 'get a course on the Internet', there are several textbooks on this conversion process, or discuss it with your local computer experts. In other words, the actual process of putting material on the Internet is not that difficult, but this simple process offers limited teaching and learning outcomes.

If you want to extend the teaching and learning process through the use of the Internet, you will need to spend time and consider the options, such as Dreamweaver, Blackboard and the add ons to these development applications. What is required is a process of analysis to make sure that the materials that go on the Internet are quality teaching and learning materials that will engage the learner in meaningful teaching and learning activities. This means developing a more sophisticated view of the materials when it is translated from a face-to-face setting, or from a textbook.

Developing the new view of preparing a course for Internet delivery

One of the problems with translating face-to-face teaching into alternative modes is that the materials developed for face-to-face teaching actually lack content. These materials are structured, but in the form of a skeleton. There is agreement between the structure that appears in the teacher's handbook and the learner's workbook, but that is all that is there, a structure. The structure or skeleton is to be fleshed out by the information that the teacher's notes prompt the teacher to provide to the learner, in the class. The learner's notes will be fleshed out by the information provided by the teacher, in the class. As a result, if you take the teacher handbook and the learner workbook you end up with a structural view of the course without content. But at least you have a structure and that is a starting point.

The preferred starting point is with a 'clean sheet' of paper; reversioning or revisioning existing materials is full of problems. With the clean sheet of paper, the objectives, learning outcomes and competency statements associated with the course can be laid out. If you have a view of what the learner is to achieve, then you should be able to work through the content and develop a structure for the information in the course based on the attributes.

The ability to structure the content based on the outcomes for the learners is one means of creating more sophisticated teaching and learning materials. This is discussed later in this chapter. Briefly, a further level of analysis of the course material will lead to the possibility of identifying attributes for the information in the course. This could be a schematic diagram of the relationship between elements in the course material. This development of a set of attributes will provide a more meaningful framework for the information (or content) of that attribute and the relationship to learners' current knowledge. In particular it will open possibilities for the learner to navigate the material. What follows is a listing of the most common attributes of course material. These attributes relate to the content, the means of exposition of the content and the instructional devices that represent the manner of exploring the content. In giving course material an attribute you are verifying that the information has a place in the course. You are also making apparent the relationship between components of the course for the learner.

The Internet and instructional design: attributes of the content

It is assumed that course design and outcomes should relate to national training agenda statements and requirements such as NVQs in the UK or similar standards such as the Australian Vocational Training Standards (AVTS), Key Competencies in language, maths, the sciences and the arts, evolving in countries around the world. If you are planning and preparing an existing course for delivery on the Internet, an underlying assumption is that the instructional design considerations for this course have been undertaken and will be appropriate for the Internet. If this is not the case then there is a need to identify the attributes in the course and the appropriate teaching and learning strategies or instructional devices and relate them to the outcomes sought by accrediting agencies and the learners.

Most learners using the Internet are 'schooled' in the use of course attributes; their schooling was formal. For these people, with a variety of learning styles, to use a textbook involves certain behaviours of access from linear (starting at page one) to eclectic (using the table of contents and index as a means of finding the information they need). It is tempting to use the same paradigm for course material to be delivered on the Internet. This fits neatly with the current vogue to publish on the Internet.

A course has contents and attributes

The course contents have attributes that enable the information in the course to be identified. This identification process can then be matched to the attributes that promote learning in a meaningful manner. One way of identifying the attributes of a course is to deconstruct it into the identifying elements. The terminology will vary in different educational and training settings, but one means of doing this is as follows.

A *course* is made up of *subjects* and / or *modules*. These subjects will have parts or *sections*. Within these sections there may be one or several *concepts* that form the basis of the section.

This is one way of deconstructing the content and providing the *elements of information* to form the basis of an Internet version of the content. For example:

An element of information
An element of information could be as small as a *sentence* or as large as a *section*; it could be a *definition*. In most cases, however, an element of information will be a *paragraph* or a *sequence of paragraphs containing a single concept*. There may be *relationships* with other paragraphs that give added meaning. It is identifying these elements and determining the links or relationship with other concepts or activities that should provide a dynamic presentation of information to assist learners to follow their investigations and learn.

While there are attributes to the course, there are also attributes to delivering a course. This will require consideration of instructional strategies to optimize the use of the technology being used.

Instructional attributes or devices

If the course you are dealing with already exists, an underlying assumption is that the instructional design considerations for this course have been undertaken. In other words, the needs, expected outcomes and information and tasks for the learner have been identified and appropriate teaching and learning information and activities along with assessment tasks have been developed. This may not directly translate to an Internet delivery. At the same time, if you are developing a new course for delivery via the Internet then you will need to undergo an analysis process for the course and the use of the Internet outlined earlier.

To present material on the Internet as a learning tool we should be incorporating all those features that optimize computer-based learning and reduce to a minimum those features that have already been identified as hindering learning through the use of computers.

It is likely that there are five styles of presentation. These styles would accommodate the delivery of content taking into account the attributes of the content. These attributes can be classified as:

Theory
    concept to examples
    concrete to abstract
    case studies
Preparation for practice
Simulation and
Problem solving

One of the main features of making Internet-based learning attractive is developing the interaction with the teaching and learning materials.

Strengths

The strengths of computer-based education and training that might be brought to an Internet delivery are as follows:

Educational

- Ability to work on course at a time convenient to the learner improves motivation.

- The 'patience' of the computer when testing and re-testing learners for appropriate drill and knowledge.

- Structured nature of computer-based materials gives learners the view of the content as a professional would view it.

- Ability to provide simulations prior to real-world experience provides a learning environment and saves expensive equipment or consumables.

- Segments of course offered on computer provide variety, may stimulate learners and promote positive attitudes to learning.

- Courses originating from a central source mean that content versions are minimized, quality is controllable, and reporting, evaluation and record keeping may be facilitated.

- A degree of individualized instruction is possible (particularly if the learner is able to navigate the content).

- When properly constructed, the computer-based learning is able to provide almost instant feedback.

A further consideration provided by the Internet is the ready availability of links to other sources of information and the ability to send messages. For example, in an engineering course it is possible to point the learner to catalogues or at least e-mail addresses as a source of information for the learner to complete his or her task.

Weaknesses

Educational

- Putting material that is not appropriate into the computer (electronic page turning). Possibly this is related to design issues.

- Interactivity requires both the learner and the notional teacher to actively use the facilities and options provided, and sometimes this does not happen. If there is no interaction there is no communication; but more importantly, this is evidence of no commitment to the use of technology.

Technical

- Limitations such as computer power or screen size or ability of operating system to cope.

Devices

To make the information interactive will require the use of a combination of one or more of the following devices. These should be used as appropriate and in a meaningful relation with the elements of information within the teaching and learning materials. They should be used in a uniform manner in a course or suite of courses. In principle, the devices provide a focus for the learner, access to information about available teaching and learning materials and a means of accessing the material in a teaching and learning context that has the potential for accreditation for the learner on completion of the learning tasks.

These devices are:

- statements of objectives, competencies to be achieved and outcome statements;
- consultations with learners or representatives to determine expected outcomes;
- definitions of terms and concepts;
- sequencing instruction, to follow the practice of the expert;
- embedding organizers in the text to place (situate) the new material with the knowledge and skills already held by the learner and to allow or encourage the learner to explore;
- placement of questions and prompts to encourage learning behaviour;
- providing maps (road maps or flow diagrams) of the content, making relationships between concepts apparent or possible courses of action apparent;
- illustrations, graphs and graphics, photographs and audio and video;
- assessment methods;
- visual signposts, icons, headings, highlighting and pop-ups;
- tables;
- simulation and virtual reality;
- practical/workshop/hands on.

Generally, attributes or devices work in the following ways.

Statements of objectives, competencies to be achieved and outcome statements

Statements of objectives, competencies and outcomes inform course developers of the information required for the learner to achieve the outcomes. If these are made known to the learner they provide the learner with clues about the direction of their inquiry and the information they seek. Making these statements available encourages the learner to consider their current knowledge and skill levels. This encourages the learner and the teaching institute or industrial enterprise to focus on what the learner knows and what they need to know.

Consultations with learners or representatives

This allows the learners to define their learning requirements. In doing so they also start on the learning process. I have included the term representative here because in some cases, at the enterprise level management and employee representatives may also be stakeholders in the education and training process. In a different case it could be parents, carers or partners who have a legitimate role in the negotiated learning process.

Definitions of terms and concepts

Definitions are discrete information. A definition may be the lowest common denominator as an element of information. In the Internet context of hyperlinks it may also form a point of departure on an exploration of the related teaching and learning materials or an extended search for related information on the Internet.

Sequencing instruction: relationships between elements of knowledge and skills

It is possible to sequence information. The rule to remember is: what does the learner need to know before they can come to terms with this new information? How is this knowledge or skill information related to existing knowledge or skills?

Embedding organizers in the text

Organizers are sections of text that tell the learner what they are about to be shown as learning materials.

One form of organizer is the advance organizer; this is a summary of the work the learner is about to see. In an Internet delivery this would contain 'hot-spots' to allow interaction and facilitate navigation.

The accepted organizers of a table of contents and an index are also available for Internet delivery of teaching and learning material. Again it will be the links created from the table of contents or the index that make the Internet material accessible to the learner.

Placement of questions and prompts encouraging learning behaviour

Questions should be set into the text, or other means of delivery, that relate directly to the information the learner has just seen and for them to answer at that point. This should serve to embed the new information in the mind of the learner.

Prompts are statements that inform the learner that they should recall prior information to use with the new information that is about to be presented to them.

Providing maps (road maps or flow diagrams) of the content, making relationships between concepts apparent

In all courses it should be possible to map the relationship of the concepts in relation to each other. A 'simplified' version of that map may assist a learner with conceptualizing not only the relationship but what they have learnt, how it fits in with other concepts and what is still to be learnt. A map could be a flow diagram.

As print material, teaching and learning information has a linear sequence, although it is possible to access the information by randomly flicking through the pages of the text. In an Internet version of material it might be advisable to provide a concept map of the information to inform learners where they are in the information and what information they should access next. This could be in the form of a diagram that alters as major sections of the work are accessed. For example, Figure 4.1 might be the map a learner sees at an early stage of the course.

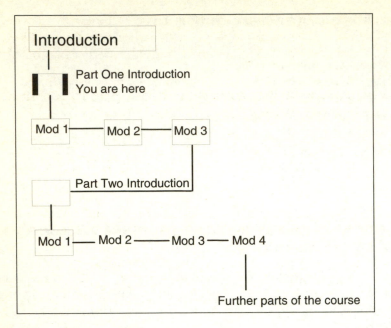

Figure 4.1   Course map 1

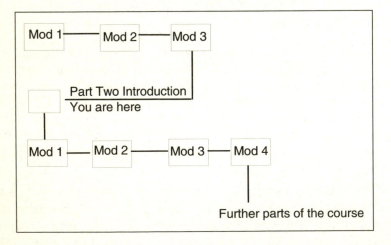

Figure 4.2   Course map 2

This would change to the map shown in Figure 4.2 after the learner has completed the modules (mod) of part one. In reality the map would change when the learner reached each identified module or part of the course.

Illustrations, graphs and graphics, photographs and audio and video

On the Internet it is possible for teaching and learning materials to contain these non-text elements. One major consideration will be what problems might be caused to the learner if their machine is not powerful enough or suitably equipped to cope with the demands of a video clip. It is also important that the illustration, video clip (audio-visual element) is linked into the text material and the teaching and learning purpose of the material. While this is a technology problem there are possible solutions such as allowing the learner to download the whole file through their browser. This should enable them to 'run' the file from their hard disk through their browser. I would also point out that the Internet is an evolving entity and with advances in compression technology, the problems of graphics, audio and video will be yesterday's problems.

Assessment methods

Assessment methods are another device through which learners organize their learning activities. This starts with the learners' concerns about what will be in the test or examination, but is also determined by the need to make submissions during the learning process. Therefore learners may make use of assessment advice as a means of organizing their learning.

Visual signposts

In many distance education and open learning texts *icons* are used to indicate to the learner that information, stills and video are associated with the current material. In these cases the icons refer to some material not in the printed text. In an Internet-delivered course some of this information will be available on screen. Clicking on the icon should reveal or *pop-up* the hidden information, visual/audio clip, etc. This hidden material may have other information associated with it.

Headings provide textual clues to the learner. For example, these three sets of headings indicate (or should indicate) the level of importance of the information contained under the heading. In most cases a set of headings as set out below will contain the following:

First order or major heading
The key concept or main point(s)
Second order or section headings
Supporting points or illustrative material
Third order or sub-headings
Tease out the more subtle points that are the difference between pretender and expert.

Highlighting of text can assist learners; however, if it is to be used as a navigation tool or an indicator of further 'hidden' information, the use of highlighting must be consistent.

Tables

These may be used to provide information or as part of a worked example or an assessment task. In an Internet delivery the use of tables could be a downloaded task, an interactive task or a developmental task to be submitted. In the downloaded or developmental task, the learner would, over a period of time, construct a table of comparisons to illustrate the learner's comprehension of variations. In the interactive task a learner would be dealing in real time with the information in the table. In this sense the table would be providing a simulation.

Simulation and virtual reality

A simulation is an event where a learner is presented with information and is able to input responses or information to achieve an outcome. For example, there are computer-based learning packages for training in the use of spreadsheets. When a learner uses one of these packages and is successful, these results need to be recorded. The outcome should be able to be matched against a 'correct' or 'range of correct' answers. In more sophisticated forms the simulation may use animation, audio and video clips. The move into virtual reality is simulation with greater degree of reality. The costs of moving into virtual reality will be related to the complexity of the simulation.

Increasingly it will be possible to use simulation, particularly if course designers are able to see the educational need. Developers will need to overcome the desire to develop a virtual reality 'star wars' bent, and to produce 3D walkthroughs that will act as vicarious learning experiences. Already it is possible to work in the real world as a simulation using real data with real outcomes. However, it is safer in an educational and training environment to be isolated from the real world for training purposes. At the very least this means that simulation virtual working does not corrupt the real transactions.

Practical/workshop/hands on

As I write this, I would have to say that the monitoring of practicals to provide the sanctioning of learning on the Internet is possible. However, when planning the materials and it is apparent that practical activities are required, there will be a need for this requirement to be addressed and a realistic solution to be referred to in the material. This means notifying learners about:

- the assessment of these activities;

- when and how the assessments are scheduled;

- how to arrange to be assessed;

- whether assessment means attending an assessment centre.

Evaluation tasks

Using the Internet as a teaching and learning tool requires a modification on the approach taken for assessing learner progress in face-to-face teaching. Learners using the Internet may be ready to undertake assessment tasks at different times. This raises the obvious need to have a range of tests available to overcome the possibility of learners comparing tests.

The most appropriate type of evaluation tasks for the Internet involves the use of *check the correct answer/multiple choice* type activities. The reason is that these types of test items allow for a large number of variant test items to be developed relating to specific learning outcomes and the ability of these to be placed in a random test generator. It also allows the responses to be corrected automatically and the results 'posted' to the electronic record of the learner held by the institution and to the teacher and the learner for their information.

Where the use of *free text* is required, as in a short answer or comment or short essay, these types of responses are best treated as mail messages and directed to the person responsible for evaluating the answers. Currently the development of a thesaurus to cope with free text responses is too time consuming for a cost–benefit effect over the scanning of the text by the person responsible for assessing the response submitted by the learner.

Reporting

In part this is covered in evaluation tasks above. There are three audiences for *reports* on learner progress. These are the learner, the teacher and the enrolling institution records. If a learner is using Internet delivery these three audiences remain. However, the collection of information should be developed so that there are a minimum of extra actions required by the learner, the teacher and the institution to maintain records of the learner's activities, the outcomes and current status. For example, is it possible to forward the results of a learner's submission after it has been assessed, either through a computer-based records management system application or via the assessor to the teacher, the enrolling institution records data base and the learner?

Communications

Forms, e-mail, phone, fax and snail mail. Forms fall into three categories, each designed so that the learner is able to submit information in a manner that is uniform for the purpose. The three generic forms are:

- enquiry / enrolment;
- submission of structured test items / multiple choice / selection;
- request / free text / submission.

In the era of electronic forms it is preferable to have one form that evolves, rather than a proliferation of forms that mimic the numerous paper forms required in the past. The fields that you develop for these forms will follow a pattern. All forms will contain fields for names and contact details. However, when a learner enrols further information fields are added. These will include unique learner identifier, course name, code, teacher involved/contact person/contact position. Note: on enquiry/enrolment forms it is better to have a contact position such as enrolling officer, rather than the name of a particular person, because people move more regularly than positions change.

Enquiry/enrolment

Forms for enrolment may have fields for preference of course (if offered) and should include personal detail capture fields for information such as addresses and telephone contacts. It may be an advantage to include fields that allow the capture of information for statistical or reporting purposes to funding bodies such as government departments. This of course raises other issues of confidentiality.

Submission of structured test items/multiple choice/selection

Forms for structured test items as well as identification fields will also have fields for questions. These questions should be able to be generated from an item bank. Questions generated from an item bank require verification of validity. The item bank needs to be large enough to enable random generation of items with variety to cover the course in order for all learners to receive a set of questions that contain similar degrees of difficulty while maintaining a variety in challenge to the learner.

These forms should also have the capability of being passed through an evaluation application for scoring purposes.

Request/free text/submission

Forms for non-standard requests and free text answers should be able to be submitted to the appropriate teacher through an *e-mail* style facility. In the case of these forms it will be the responsibility of the teacher to respond to the request or assess the free text answers.

The use of *fax* and *phone* contacts and *snail mail* or the *postal service* should not be overlooked as alternative means of communication. Some of these forms of communication may serve the learner's needs better than a dogmatic need to comply with computer-based communication.

Video and audio

This is the most rapidly developing area of the Internet. Consideration will need to given if video and audio form part of the course materials. Given the wide range of computer configurations it is difficult to make a prescriptive guide. However, in the immediate future, it may be more appropriate to distribute high-quality video and audio by cassette through the post than have learners using low-speed modem lines. However, the use of emerging desktop video systems (at a cheap price [under A$600]) should not be discounted, particularly as most new computers are being delivered with sound and video cards. These desktop video and audio systems use the technology developed for 'Stump Cam' in cricket, 'Fender Cam' or 'Helmet Cam' in motor racing and yachting. The cameras serve as both face cameras and document cameras.

The current technology has been criticized as it is seen as slow scan screen refresh. However, if the critics could look beyond their 'It's not as good as broadcast' mentality they would see that there are attributes of slow refresh time. For a start, the use of this video can be used in the following settings:

- face-to-face;
- demonstrations;
- explorations.

Face-to-face

The use of desktop video through the Internet could be used for various interview settings. These could be for a job, pre-court hearings with alleged criminals, or between peers in a course, or a course participant seeking information from an expert.

Demonstrations

One criticism of the current video standard is that it blurs movement. In my opinion it is a strength. For example, the blurring of movement in a demonstration allows me to see the path of the hand as it moves through the demonstration.

Explorations

In an interactive setting the blurring motion allows me to sit back and check the thinking of the learner as they work through the problem and vocalize and demonstrate their enquiry process, to which I have to respond. A less viable alternative solution but still with educational effect is to incorporate captured stills into the information with links in the text of a generic HTML presentation. The advent of an application such as 'Hot Java' is an indication of things to come in terms of interaction, simulation and communication.

Of course the wider distribution of servers should mean that this information can be downloaded to a local (campus) server, increasing the learner's access at minimal connect cost. However, this leaves open the question on selecting appropriate material for delivery using the Internet as a tool.

Selection of appropriate course content

In determining the type of course to be presented / delivered on the Internet there are two possibilities. The first is that the course material already exists, the second that the course material needs to be developed. In the discussion that follows there are two scenarios based on the existence of the course.

One scenario is that there are existing course materials, which means that the analysis of the needs, outcomes and content have been agreed. These assumptions need to be reassessed in relation to delivery of the materials on the Internet. If the course materials and content are appropriate, there are still the issues of how best to utilize the attributes of the Internet and to explore other options where it is apparent that the Internet is not suited as a means of delivery.

The second scenario is that the course does exist but the materials are not in a form that is readily transferable to an Internet delivery. Therefore there are no materials. This raises the question of how an Internet delivery might be developed that is beneficial to teachers, learners and the community when developed.

This section examines the following issues:

- How do you determine if a course could be suited to development and delivery on the Internet?

- Sequencing information: the book as a model.
- Elements of information (possible attributes).
- Page content and links within and between pages.
- Considerations about course materials.

How do you determine if a course could be suited to development and delivery on the Internet?

In educational and training organizations most of the accredited course material currently available is in print form and a skeletal outline. It is the teachers who translate the outline into classroom teaching and learning outcomes. There is an expectation that a teacher working in a classroom will interpret the curriculum documents and present their version of the course with a combination of diagrams, illustrations and photographs, perhaps with a supporting video. How is this transferred to the Internet?

The short answer is that it is possible to transfer everything to the Internet. However, to do so is to fall into the worst trap of electronically delivered material, namely to create course materials that are electronic page turning with none of the features to encourage learning in a computer environment.

The question you need to ask is: what is the internal logic of the course material that learners need to know? To answer that question you will need to consider the following:

- How are the outcomes for learners, the objectives, the competencies expected for the learner stated? If these are obvious, you will then have to determine how the content of the course can be given attributes.
- You will have to determine attributes for the information.
- You will have to determine the links between these elements of information.

At the beginning of this chapter it was stated that a course is made up of subjects and/or modules. These subjects will have parts (sections). Within these sections there may be one or several concepts that form the basis of the section. These can be the means of deconstructing the print version and providing the elements to build the Internet version of the content. To build the Internet version you will need to develop an unique identifier to

Level One	Title of a course is similar to a textbook title
	Lists of subjects or modules in a course are similar to the table of contents in a textbook
	Contents in subjects and modules of a course are similar to contents of chapters or sections in a textbook
Level Two	In current course materials it is rare to have an index of contents similar to a textbook
Level Three	There may be references in a course and these are similar to references in a textbook

Figure 4.3   Structure in print materials

cover for each of the elements of the course content. The reason for identifying these attributes is that it enables a more flexible enquiry routine (almost like the routine of using an index in a book) by the learner. This flexible enquiry should support the learner in charge of their learning. One way of comparing existing print materials to materials for the Internet is shown in Figure 4.3.

Sequencing information: the book as a model

If the analogy of a book is used then the similarities, shown in Figure 4.3, between presenting a course on the Internet and a book arise.

To a large extent the major difference between preparing material for a book and preparing information for the Internet is to be found at Level Two. If you want to prepare information for the Internet as a traditional course a major consideration will be to determine the finite bits of information and develop the relationship and attributes these bits of information may need to take. The activity that needs to be undertaken by a person or team seeking to place learning materials on the Internet is to determine a sequence or links between the information to allow the learner access to information, and to consider alternative pathways to allow for individual learning difference needs or information requirements.

However, if the intention is to provide a source of information and to allow the enquirer or learner to develop their own meaning, the team will need to develop a different set of attributes and a learner-centred means of dealing with the interactions required.

Elements of information (possible attributes)

An element of information could be as small as a sentence or as large as a section. In most cases, however, an element of information will be a paragraph or a sequence of paragraphs containing a single concept. There may be relationships with other paragraphs that give added meaning.

In developing a face-to-face presentation for learners, the intention is to identify these elements and determine the links that should provide a dynamic presentation of information and enable the learner to learn. In order to build the Internet version with a teacher-to-learner orientation, you will need to develop an identifier unique to each of the elements in the material. The attributes will include those of *heading*, or *definition*, or *reading*, or *activity*, or *revision*, amongst others. Labelling that element of information with an attribute does not mean that it is uniquely identified. After all, there may be many elements of information within a course with the attribute *heading*. To further define the element, it (the element) will need to have a relationship to other information elements and the attributes of those elements. This is also important for the presentation on screen. If the presentation of the course material is to be dominated by the institution then there are some considerations of labelling the elements to lock the structure. Essentially these are similar to computer-based learning strategies. In this setting the designers of the course will want to label and make links between labels so that the structure of the course follows the understanding of the subject matter expert.

In this context, if you plan to design the presentation you will follow a path as follows.

Page content and links within and between pages

If you are planning a teacher/subject expert delivery of course materials you will need to identify each specific element of content. There are many ways of doing this identification. The important point for developers is to maintain the protocol of identification during the planning, development and delivery process.

As an example, it is possible for the course developers to create a set of identifiers for information in a course or activities in a course and provide information about the links so that a programmer is able to prepare a course and the links between these elements in a course. This will mean the development of a set of codes so that the cross-links between pages of information are documented. The reason for this documentation may seem trivial when you first develop the information, but the documentation will become very important if there is a subsequent need to revise the course.

For example:

- a code 'S' for learner/general information or 'T' exclusively for teacher information;

- a code for the course, eg 'UBW' for Underwater Basket Weaving;

- a code for the module, eg 'HYB' for the module Hold Your Breath;

- a unique code for the element of information. This might be a logical reference to the location of the material in the original information.

As a result you arrive at a code for a specific piece of information such as SUBWHYB004, where 004 is the location of the information. Another piece of information might be identified as SUBWKNT004; in this instance much of the identifier seems the same except for the code change KNT. This indicates that the information comes from the KNT module of the course.

This type of identifying and cross-referencing is fine if the product is to be a computer-based education and training package and for the 'programmer' developing the package, but what about the learners? Do they want to know that they need to address SUBWHYB004 in order to get information from the KNT part of the course?

In an enquiry-driven version of a course on the Internet learners are looking for materials that they can utilize to build their skills for their immediate need. For these people the navigational devices need to be menus and perhaps icons and hot spots in text to allow them to work their way through the material. This working may seem haphazard to a teacher if it does not follow the learning path the teacher expected. Given the 'model' of the Internet as source of information, with the learners making of that information what they will, the haphazard, eclectic activities of learners are only able to be evaluated against a consideration of whether the learners achieved what they set out to do, and this may or may not be for formal recognition. For these people recognition of current skills, consideration of former and formal learning and access to courses to develop a skill set are important only to the extent that they improve their skills, increase the possibility of employment options, or gain recognition for qualifications or satisfy a whim.

Considerations about course materials

Most courses consist of practical and theoretical components. Even the most academic courses require the learner to submit a practical submission, such as an essay, to indicate a grasp of the content and to demonstrate their capabilities in arguing/handling the content of the subject. If you are considering developing a version of the course for delivery through the Internet, you will need to determine how you will handle these aspects of the course.

In my opinion there is a mistaken belief that the handling of theoretical material seems less of a problem. There seems to be a general opinion that course developers for an Internet delivery will initially want to consider how they will handle the practical aspects of the course. If I follow the line of argument that dealing with practical activities is an issue in delivery of course material on the Internet then the following considerations may arise.

Practicals

Where a course has a practical component, you will need to decide what actions the learner needs to take to demonstrate that he or she is competent. In the first instance, consideration should be given to including information about the objectives and expected outcomes and assessment scheme of any practical work as a guide within the theoretical component. This could also include information for the learner to seek advance standing either through recognition of current abilities or through recognition of equivalent studies.

You will need to ask the question

You will need to consider if the learners need to attend a weekend session or after-hours session to demonstrate their practical abilities. You may consider that there are other options that are equally valid and open as an assessment to enable a learner to demonstrate their competencies. Some of these may seem radical but they may form an option that is both valid and economical for the learner and the teacher.

For example:

- Is it possible to present a simulation scenario to encourage the learner to practice prior to, or as remediation after, a practical?

- Is it possible for the learner to bring examples of their work from the workplace?

- Is it possible for the learner's workplace supervisor to provide a statement about the ability of the learner?

These are directly related to practical components of a course and may fit in with other aspects of course delivery being promoted by the educational and training institution, such as:

- granting of advanced standing;

- recognition of prior learning;

- accelerated progression.

The important consideration, at the design stage of any delivery, but in this case an Internet delivery, is how to devise activities within the Internet delivery to sanction the practical components of a course.

An example: how would you get learners working through the Internet to demonstrate they could carry out 'mouth-to-mouth' resuscitation?

(a) They write out a check list.

(b) They demonstrate in front of an adult.

(c) They demonstrate in front of a supervisor.

(d) They demonstrate in front of a person with first aid qualifications.

But

(e) What happens if the learner already has a first aid certificate?

Or

(f) What happens if you examine other areas of the course or the expressed interest of the learner and find out that they need to do bandages, lifting of casualties, suppression of bleeding?

If the requirement of the learner is general first aid then none of (a), (b) or (c) serves a purpose. The option (d) could overcome the immediate verification problem, but what of the other learner needs?

The part of the scenario at (e) seems to be straightforward: give them recognition for prior learning. However, before that can happen there will need to be actions to determine that the prior qualifications reflect current practices and standards, and that the learner is a competent practitioner, not just a holder of a certificate – in other words, they are up to date.

The opportunity offered by scenario (f) includes requiring the learner to complete a first aid course that satisfies all the requirements and to recognize this as equivalent to at least the practical part of the course or learner's need and accelerate the progression of the learner.

It is also important that considerations about enabling the learner to demonstrate practical skills are related to the underlying concepts or theory. In an Internet delivery of a course there will need to be consideration about the form of presentation of the theory. There is the paradigm of classroom or didactic presentation represented by teachers, presenters and gate-keepers of knowledge. There is also the more eclectic, enquiry-based consideration of learners as active negotiators in developing access to the learning/information they require.

Considerations for the theoretical components of the course

In the classroom, using a whiteboard and felt pen or only using overheads (chalk and talk) is not the most stimulating means of conveying theory. The use of the Internet requires that a selection process takes place.

Some of the questions you will need to ask about presenting the theory component of a course or a theory-based course are:

- What in this material is most appropriate for presentation/delivery to learners by the Internet, ie a computer?

- What in the content will promote interaction with the content?

- What in the content requires learner input such as selection from multiple choice possibilities?

- Most of the course material currently available is in print form, perhaps with a supporting video. How is this transferred to the Internet?

If you assume that the Internet is an open learning space and you are using the Internet as a delivery tool, then the following questions should be answered by you as a developer. As stated earlier, a needs analysis should have provided you with answers to questions such as:

- Who might be searching for your information?

- How do you sanction any learning or 'claim' to learning?

Then there are considerations of the learner

If a learner is going to access teaching and learning materials through a computer, then certain considerations at the planning stage might assist the learner. I can only write the obvious here: I consider a help facility that offers no help to be no help.

Then there are the possibilities of supporting accelerated progression of the learner. This aspect of the use of the Internet needs to be explored. It seems to me that with course material available on the Internet a learner might be able to take at least two actions to improve their standing within the course. The first of these is to request and, after submission of documents, achieve recognition for prior learning, or work-related learning that links to the course. One feature that recognition systems are keen to promote is that prior learning or experience will be taken into account to break the traditional time-serving structure of education and training. However, as a generalization, the overlay of documentation to 'prove' prior learning or experience and a grant of recognition seems to be more than attending the course or subject. Yet through an appropriate Internet interface much of this documentation could be easily managed.

A second possibility is that the learner could elect for a pre-test. This pre-test would cover aspects of the course. On submitting the results and after analysis the learner would be forwarded a report about their study needs in relation to the course. This might serve as a means of accelerating some learners through the course. The use of such tests might also include the use of simulations, where the simulation gives a wider perspective on the capability of the learner.

A further aid to the learner would be to provide them (and you) with an audit trail of what the learner accessed prior to taking the test to determine if the learner failed because of bad access skills on their part, bad design on your part or what the learner needs to do as remediation.

Another consideration for the learner is access time costs. If the learner is working with a local server, then time costs are minimal but important. If the learner is working from a remote site, consideration should be given to the ability to download the material. This will mean considerations of security of the materials and of the learner's interaction back to the site.

Course delivery on the Internet

The Internet is 'promoted' as a superhighway of information. In reality it is a conduit for people seeking information and/or course materials. The Internet is not neutral as a conduit in that the performance available to the person using the Internet is a product of the design of the course material, the computer power supporting that material and the computer power of the learner's own computer.

The facility of the Internet is also dependent on the type of browser and enquiry structures available to the learner. Your course design for presentation on the Internet might not be very user-friendly if the user is accessing the course on a slow modem, with a different browser and from the opposite side of the country or hemisphere.

There is also an issue of confidence for the promoters of a course, institutions offering course materials and the learners seeking access. Each of these will be questioning the credibility of a course delivered by the Internet. In any new venture or means of course delivery there will be the doubts about the material and the means of delivery. The question to be asked by all developers is: will it work? This is an understandable question of confidence.

In the short term, developers of courses for delivery via the Internet will have to face the question of confidence not only of the process but of the outcomes in any course development and delivery setting. When it comes to the use of the Internet as a delivery tool there are different perspectives. The current mythology of the Internet is that it is an open access computer-based enquiry and messaging system. This is interpreted by the public as open access to information. But what if learners want accreditation? How will they respond if they are asked to provide evidence about their current skills to satisfy competency standards? How will they react if this information is to be recorded?

There are two assumptions you can make. The first is that learners accessing your site and information may not require recognition or accreditation. They came, they saw and they went away contented. This may have implications for how you see your intellectual property rights. The second is that learners will seek some form of acknowledgement for accessing your material. At this point, records and results and course fee considerations come to the fore. You will need to consider these aspects sooner rather than later, not the least reason being the need to think about security arrangements for learners submitting responses to course requirements and personal information including addresses, credit card numbers and phone numbers.

Confidence

Assuming that there is an audience for your information and the mechanisms for sanctioning the learning outcomes, if learners use the course materials on the Internet, then it is still possible that questions will be raised about the use of the Internet as a teaching and learning space. This is a question of confidence in the use of the Internet as a delivery tool. This is generally raised by those with a conservative approach to education. By the way, it is a question of confidence that can be raised about any non-face-to-face delivery method.

Ask yourself the following about a learner using a course delivered face-to-face:

- Did the learner pass the test?

- Did the learner pass the questions set in the test?

- Did all the questions cover all aspects of the content?

Now, are you prepared to say that the learner is knowledgeable? In reality the question is about the testing procedure, not the method of delivery or the learner's ability.

Further confidence test: the learner failed the knowledge test that he or she filled in on an electronic form on a computer in his or her workplace. However, the learner completed the practical tasks competently. Are you prepared to say that the learner is not competent?

I recognize that these cases seem to be comparing chalk and cheese, but the problem is real. The problem is one of perceptions about learners learning and the sanctioning of that learning when it is undertaken in other than conventional settings. I suspect that for many in the educational and training community, learning using the Internet is another alternative beyond the barely/grudgingly accepted means of course delivery by correspondence.

Conclusion

There is a growing experience of delivering courses via the Internet, one option is to look at similar experiences in delivering courses. The logical choice is that of course delivery by computer. One expectation is that the same strengths and weaknesses that apply to computer-based learning will apply to most aspects of teaching and learning on the Internet.

The strengths of computer-based education and training that might be brought to an Internet delivery include, amongst others:

- the ability to work on the course at a time convenient to the learner, either online or by downloading a course or components to be worked on in real-time standalone run time;

- the structured nature of computer-based materials providing the learner with a professional view of the content;

- the provision of simulations prior to real-world experience;

- possibility of individualized instruction;

- Internet learning is capable of providing almost instant feedback.

These strengths are further enhanced when the Internet has ready availability of links to other sources of information and the ability to send messages.

There are weaknesses, and these include:

- putting inappropriate material on the Internet;

- both the learner and the notional teacher need actively to use the facilities and options provided. Sometimes this does not happen. If there is no interaction there is no communication. If there is no communication it is difficult to verify that learning is taking place.

However, these are not the only considerations. Currently there are available computer-based tools that allow the direct conversion of a word-processed file to pages on the Internet. In my opinion, more than just a simple conversion is needed to make text material suitable for educational and training use on the Internet. What is required is a process of analysis to make sure that the materials that go on the Internet are quality teaching and learning materials, that will engage the learner in meaningful teaching and learning activities. This means developing a more sophisticated structure to the materials.

Structuring the content on the basis of intended learning outcomes or objectives is one means of creating more sophisticated teaching and learning materials. A further level of analysis of the course material will lead to the possibility of identifying attributes for the information in the course. It is the development of a set of attributes that will provide a more meaningful framework for the information (or content) of that attribute. These attributes or the relationship between attributes will indicate ways of presenting the content and the instructional devices that represent the manner of exploring the content. These, along with the requirement of the learner, are indicators of how material could be presented to satisfy course presentation and the enquiry of an individual learner.

For general considerations of course development see Forsyth *et al* (1999) *Planning, Development, Delivery* and *Evaluation of a Course* (four titles, Kogan Page, London). These are four interrelated books that consider the issues at each stage of course development and delivery. The books address the issues of analysis and materials production that you will need to consider for any means of course delivery, including the use of the Internet.

5 Cost considerations, economic benefits and budget

Summary

Placing any course on the Internet will involve some costs. There will be costs of providing a course delivery service on campus, within a multi-campus institution, and to allow access to the course material by people outside the institution. There may be cost for the learners and there may be benefits for teachers, learners and the institution. It is difficult to place a monetary value on some of these aspects. However, budgets do have to be prepared and used.

For an institution setting out to offer a course on the Internet, the question must be how much the institution is willing to spend (or is it invest?) to set up the course. The investment will have a value, but there are investments in kind and it is in these investments in kind or goodwill investments of staff that could affect the outcomes of course delivery. For example, it is relatively easy and therefore cheap to run a generic mark-up language over a Word file and then claim that you have a course on the Internet (having set up your WWW site, etc). However, over the last five years of monitoring these sites, such a cheap adaptation to the Internet means that learners using the course are likely to be faced with long scrolled pages of text on screen or incessant mouse clicks as they scroll through pages of course information. In the long run, this cheap and quick solution leads to dissatisfaction by the learner and the material will be ignored. As such, the cost of establishing the site will not be amortized by people visiting the site or taking up the learning materials. As a result, the capital costs of file servers, local (LAN) and wide area (WAN) network considerations and the costs of developing even the cheapest version of a course for the Internet will be difficult to justify.

At the moment, a modest Internet site can run off a fairly powerful personal computer with modem and large disk space to handle the expected flood of enquiries and course participants. That is the minimum. More powerful personal computers and improved communications through ISDN (Integrated Services Digital Network) (digital telephone lines) and even the compression technologies, using the plain old telephone system (POTS) with ADSL (Asymmetric Digital Subscriber Loop), may increase the performance of your site, but the ultimate guide to performance of your site will be the power of the equipment available to the learner.

There will also be costs associated with providing a service on campus and of access by people who have no affiliation with the institution, until they sign up for the Internet-delivered course.

For the learner the costs could be minimal and associated directly with access to the course materials. However, the cost could be considerable if the learner is paying for hardware (computer, modem etc) and connect time. Just as cost considerations fall into two main areas for the institution and costs for the learner, benefits are available to both the institution and the learner.

This chapter looks at a generic set of possible costs and benefits under the following headings:

- costs for institutions;
- costs for learners;
- benefits for institutions;
- educational benefits for learners;
- summary of cost benefits against the cost benefits for the community;
- budget considerations.

Costs for institutions

The costs for the institution fall into the following categories.

Cost/benefit of making course material available via the Internet

In part this involves considering current delivery costs and comparing these costs (assumed face-to-face teaching) with the possible and future delivery costs using the Internet.

Maintenance

In face-to-face delivery there is a capital cost of developing and maintaining the physical structures, the bricks and mortar. When these facilities are established there is the ongoing cost of maintenance alongside any need to refurbish these buildings to accommodate new courses.

Set-up costs

There are costs associated with setting up an Internet site. These should include:

- capital costs;
- cabling and connectivity costs such as software;
- systems management;
- the costs associated with the educational considerations.

Capital costs

An institution that has courses that might be suited to delivery through the Internet is an institution that has laid out a considerable amount of money for the development of those courses or resources. A question that the institution needs to resolve is how it might gain a return on that capital outlay. After all, the capital costs of equipment such as computers and printers are amortized over time. But how to gain a return from the product of the use of the computer equipment and the intellect of the teachers developing the course is a different matter.

Cabling and connectivity costs such as software

There is a conception that the Internet is *free*. This misconception needs to be addressed.

Systems management

If you and your students are going to use the Internet then you will need a computer systems manager with the flair and vision to facilitate the delivery of course material through the Internet that you seek.

The costs associated with the educational considerations

Educational and training courses are seen as a means of generating revenue to cover the cost of developing the courses and more importantly maintain the institution. The biggest problem is that some see the offering of courses on the Internet as a way of recouping capital outlay.

Recouping capital

The expenditure of funds (resources) to develop a course is a capital outlay. The return on that outlay can be determined rather crudely by dividing the capital outlay to develop the course by the number of learners who attend / complete the course. A further refinement is to amortize these costs over the number of years the course will run and the number of learners in each of the years. To this figure has to be added the appropriate costs of running the course each year. These include:

- teacher;
- room;
- lighting;
- expendable items;
- other costs;
- on-cost of teacher;
- etc.

In other words, to recoup the initial capital outlay on the course development incurs other costs and then there is the added cost of reviewing and revising the course to maintain relevance.

Copyright

One of the biggest headaches facing people placing course materials on the Internet may well be the copyright considerations. There is a huge mixture of myth and reality. The best option is: if you are using material that was produced by someone else then get copyright clearance. Even if you are convinced that your organization/institution is the holder of the copyright (because everyone uses the material), you should check it out. This type of institutional usage giving a *de facto* feeling of 'cleared for copyright use' is similar to the belief that 'If it's for education then its OK'. In fact the copyright laws are clear on what you can and cannot use and abuse in terms of other people's material.

With the development of the Internet there is a real possibility of abuse of copyright. This is to be found in the nature of the Internet, which is a place to roam to pick up ideas and to contribute. However, if you are using the Internet as a means of making course material available then perhaps the same rigour that is applied to copyright clearance in face-to-face materials or in other forms of presentation such as correspondence needs to be applied to Internet delivery.

The issues of copyright are compounded if you are revising course material for Internet delivery. The person or organization holding the copyright may feel guarded about extending the copyright to a different version of the course.

If the copyright you seek is for a new course that has been designed for Internet delivery, you may well face reluctance by some copyright holders to provide a release, even for educational and training use on the Internet. In part this reluctance may be based on the media-generated perspective of the Internet as an ephemeral thing that serious people do not do. In this respect there is a real clash of images of the Internet as an information source and the Internet as a site for surfing (OK, I wrote earlier that I would only use the term once and here it is again). The Internet has an image problem both as a source of information and with regard to the credibility of some of the information, and while this could affect a learner's confidence in an Internet-delivered course it may cause the copyright holder to consider seriously their position in granting copyright.

Cabling and connectivity costs such as software

This is a costing issue beyond the scope of this book. Except that if you are planning an Internet delivery of a course in an on-campus setting or across campuses, then someone will need to develop the plan for cabling and equipment to make it all work.

Systems management

In a best-case scenario there will be a person or persons on campus or in the institution with some computing systems operation knowledge. These people are important if you have minimal computing skills. They are the ones who can translate from the computer application (not your course) the 'user (un)friendly' instructions that you can only find by accident, are told by a friend or happen when you accidentally strike a combination of keys and as a consequence are transported into some operating system. It's a real problem that you need to consider. Effective systems management will troubleshoot any problems.

With Internet delivery of courses you may require links to other computer resources or messaging such as e-mail. A person with systems knowledge will be a benefit to your course delivery.

Costs associated with the educational considerations

This in part is an access issue. Over time, the ability of all to meet on the Internet may be solved, but I see that in the short term (and that may be too long) it will be the advantaged in society that access the Internet and gain from this access. This is a moral and societal consideration beyond the scope of this book but one that is of concern to me.

However, beyond the possible future costs to society there are some actual costs that both learners and institutions offering courses on the Internet need to consider.

Costs for learners

For the learner the costs will include:

- Any hardware and software costs to access the Internet.

- Internet connect costs through either a WAN or connection to a commercial server such as Compuserve.

- There may be costs associated with connect times or online costs. For example, a local call in Australia (as I write this) is a fixed-rate no-time-charge call. This means that connecting to a local service is a one-call cost no matter how long you are connected. However, if the service is outside the radius of a local call then timed call charges apply.

- Then there are the costs of registration or subscription to the course.

- There may be other costs associated with other materials for the course, for example print materials or a video.

- There may be costs of using the mail and phone as part of the course.

Benefits for institutions

In my opinion, the benefit for any institution of placing course material in an Internet environment is not the possible increase in the number of learners enrolling. It is possible that having courses available on the Internet will lead to an increase in enrolments; however, these increased enrolments will need to be serviced. Therefore, unless the material on the Internet leads to savings in servicing courses, any benefit may be minimal at best and at worst lead to an increased cost through course servicing.

One saving that is possible by placing the course material in an Internet environment is in the costs of maintaining the material. Once the material is in an Internet environment, the costs of revision and indeed the cost of a major revision as part of the quality assurance of the course (eg a fifth-year life of course revision) are greatly reduced.

Further benefits for an institution include cost savings engendered by the following:

- The 'patience' of the computer when testing and re-testing learners for appropriate drill and knowledge.

- The ability to provide simulations prior to real-world experience provides a learning environment and saves expensive equipment or consumables.

- Segments of the course offered on computer provide variety, may stimulate learners and promote positive attitudes to learning.

- Courses offered on the Internet in part or in whole may be accessed by learners at their place of work, a local library or local campus, or increasingly at home. This will reduce (not eliminate) the need for further investment in bricks and mortar.

- When originating from a central source, content versions are minimized, quality is controllable, and reporting, evaluation and record keeping may be facilitated.

- A degree of individualized instruction is possible (particularly if the learner is able to navigate the content). The benefit to the institution arises from the learners' perception that their needs are being satisfied.

- When properly constructed, the computer-based learning is able to provide almost instant feedback. Here again, the benefit to the institution arises from the learners' perception that their needs are being satisfied.

Educational benefits for learners

- Ability to work on a course at a time convenient to the learner improves motivation.

- The 'patience' of the computer when testing and re-testing learners for appropriate drill and knowledge.

- Structured nature of computer-based materials gives learners the view of the content as a professional would view it.

- Ability to provide simulations prior to real-world experience provides a learning environment.

- Segments of a course offered on computer provide variety, may stimulate learners and promote positive attitudes to learning.

- A degree of individualized instruction is possible (particularly if the learner is able to navigate the content).

- When properly constructed, the computer-based learning is able to provide almost instant feedback.

Summary of cost benefits against the cost benefits for the community

The use of the Internet as a delivery tool for courses increases the options for both institutions and learners in the education and training environment. However, beyond the institution and the learner are industry groups and employers, education and training agencies, other community groups ranging from grey power organizations to corrective services establishments, and individuals who are able to tap into the Internet and use these course resources, given that they satisfy enrolment criteria.

If this wider perspective of availability of course material is taken into account then the cost of developing a course for delivery by a tool such as the Internet is amortized by a significant factor. However, the cost of development and presentation is accompanied by a cost of maintenance. This cost of maintenance is hopefully not caused by users vandalizing the course material. The cost of maintenance is a legitimate cost to ensure that the course materials remain relevant.

The benefit to the community is that up-to-date course materials are available to them. The means of access to this material may be in the home, local library, at work, or in centres attached to local schools. Community members accessing material designed for the Internet will have access to interactive teaching and learning materials with the ability to communicate not only with a teacher, but peers doing the same course. In reality they will be creating their own community of learners.

Budget considerations

This section on budget considerations contains a brief description of the following major items that will form part of the expenditure of developing a course for Internet delivery:

- management;
- course revision;
- maintenance costs;
- clerical;
- staff development.

Management

As an ongoing process, a management regime is needed to ensure that the ongoing and iterative cycle of course development presentation and review is taking place. This is also part of the quality assurance process.

Course revision

This involves evaluation of course content and the development of the scheme of information elements to form the base for the course offering. This may require the following cost elements:

- subject expert;
- instructional designer;
- Internet/computer person;
- transfer and manipulation of documents;
- copyright.

Maintenance costs

Essentially these are ongoing quality assurance costs associated with maintaining information within the courses already revised. At any one time this should amount to no more than 15 per cent of the materials available on the Internet. If this 15 per cent is exceeded, a more thorough course revision is indicated. It is expected that all courses would face a major review on a five-year cycle. The costs involved will be:

- part-time subject expert/reviewer;
- person to input changes (over time, this would be a full-time position as the number of courses to be maintained increases).

An issue may arise in the revising process of the version of the course the learner is undertaking. In other words, when do you implement the revision and do you need to alert current learners that their course materials are under revision? What about the learners who have just completed the previous version – do these people need to upgrade to the new version?

Clerical

There will be clerical and on-costs associated with the presentation of material.

Staff development

There will need to be staff development activities in the following areas:

- attributes of the Internet;
- evaluation of courses for Internet delivery;
- preparing staff for flexible delivery using the Internet as a tool.

Budget structure

The budget considerations above (and probably some other considerations to deal with your local needs) generate a budget that consists of three schedules. These schedules relate to:

- estimated cost for providing courses for Internet delivery;
- the cost to learners of accessing these courses over and above any administration fee;
- an estimate of revenue generated.

Schedule 1: Internet delivery development costs

This schedule is based on expected costs in developing a one-semester course. It is assumed that on average the process to revise an already developed one-semester course will take 20 working days.

Maintenance will not take place in the first year but may be required in second and subsequent years with an absolute requirement in the fifth year and/or at the time of a major review. I have set out the chart shown in Figure 5.1 but have not included costs as these will vary from site to site.

Note 1: the costs associated with revision may be offset against the revenue generated by course fee (schedule 3).

There are other costs. I have not included any cost of using a third-party Internet gateway provider. The assumption is that you are providing your

	Personnel (per 20 days)	Notional salary	On cost	Capital item/cost	Recurrent item/cost	Other item/cost	Total
Project management	1/5 (4 days)	Manager level					
Course revision	(20 days)	Educational teaching					
Internet development	(10 days)	Internet literate					
Maintenance (at a later time)	0 (at development stage)	Educational clerical		Dedicated PC and software			
Clerical	1/5 (4 days)						
Staff development	2/5 (4 days)	Educational training		Training materials		Training support (4×1/2 day)	
Total							

Figure 5.1   Schedule 1

own Web site. If you use a third-party provider this may have some maintenance benefits and some cost savings. This third-party provider should have Internet expertise that may save your budget. However, such cost benefits will be determined by the commitment of the provider to keeping a quality site up to date.

Depending on your budget, you may be able to get outside expertise to assist you with your material on the Internet. One aspect of the process you must keep control of is the educational and training aspects of the material.

Schedule 2: learner access costs

There are likely to be three levels of cost (Figure 5.2):

- teacher/learner access on campus from a server with downloaded courseware (local access);

- teacher/learner access to courseware located at an institute level server (non-local server);

- public, teacher/learner access from outside the campus/institute network.

Schedule 3: revenue

Practical course

As an estimate, the availability of a practical course on the Internet should provide a 10 to 15 per cent increase in the availability of places on campus.

Level of access	Access type	Time	Costs
Local access	LAN/WAN on campus	LAN transaction and memory overheads apply in all levels of access. At this level is it a cost to the learner or to the department offering the course?	Course costs
Local to institute centre	Non-local server WAN access	This may be local or time-called charge depending on the external location costs to learner or department	Local and possibly distance (timed charges) between campuses of a multi-campus institution. Costs to learner that apply to the course when delivered by other methods
External	External to local or institute server	User pays local or time-called charge depending on user distance from site of course material	User pays upon enrolling to gain credit. Costs to learner that apply to the course when delivered by other methods

Figure 5.2   Schedule 2

In general, the figure is conservative because many courses have a heavy practical component requiring the use of dedicated training spaces, such as workshops. As a consequence, if it is considered unwise for the practical component to be too far in terms of time or distance from the theoretical component, the possibility of compressing a course is not as great as might be expected.

If the course is conducted at the learner's workplace, an increase in enrolments will be greater. In this case the workplace is substituting for the campus and not causing an overload on campus facilities. As a consequence, an increase of up to 50 per cent may be possible with the Internet-delivered course, using current resources. It may be difficult to increase enrolments beyond this figure without overloading teachers or employing addition resources such as teachers.

Theoretical course
When the theoretical components of the course are suited to electronic presentation and much of the practical component is suitable for computer-based simulation, it is possible that an increased availability of

places in this type of course could be as high as 50 to 80 per cent. Again this is a conservative estimate. It is based on the computer application (running underneath the Internet interface) being able to cope with most of the routine tasks, such as test and evaluation tasks, currently carried out by teachers. While this reduces the demand on teachers' time on these routine tasks, if more course places are available the full saving in routine task and face-to-face time is taken up by other teaching activities associated with the electronic delivery. For example, given the need for the teachers to interact with most learners, even if electronically, it seems reasonable to expect that activities associated with electronic teaching will replace routine tasks. These interactive activities are time consuming but are at the quality value-added end of the teaching learning process.

Potential generation of revenue arises from three sources:

1 Increased throughput of learners enables more courses to be run per semester/year.

2 Increased access to course materials enables more learners to be enrolled in any one course per semester/year.

3 Increased access to courses means that external learners are able to be charged.

The balance to be determined is the extent to which the increase in available courses or places is available for unmet demand within the institution or available to non-institution learners either directly or through the auspices of sanctioned/licensed external providers.

In all cases, there is an assumption that courses have an administrative fee component. This money reverts to the administration. It is not available to the department that generates the course. In the third case, revenue generated becomes available to the sponsors and stakeholders as per memoranda of understanding or similar types of agreement between the parties.

Example

On the assumption that a semester course to an external learner could attract a fee of A$400, Figure 5.3 indicates the level of possible revenue based on a pre-electronic delivery of 100 learners with:

- Case 1 – 10 per cent increase in places due to electronic delivery by learner access, eg the whole 10 per cent to local access or the whole 10% to external access.

Learner access	Fees generated	Fee for course	Extra places		
			Case 1 10% increase on 100 places (10) assuming all places allocated to external category	Case 2 50% increase on 100 places (50) assuming 25 to local access and 25 to external	Case 3 50% increase in places but apportioned as follows
Local access	Enrolment or admin. charge	Revenue nil	Nil	5 places nil income	20 places nil
Non-local server	Enrolment or admin. charge	Revenue nil			20 places nil
External	Admin. charge and fee for course			25 places at A$400 income	10 places at A$400 income
Total			A$4,000	A$10,000	A$4,000

Figure 5.3   Schedule 3

- Case 2 – 50 per cent increase in places due to electronic delivery, eg the whole 50 per cent to local access or the whole 50 per cent to external access.

- Case 3 – a proportion of the 50 per cent of places created being allocated across the access categories.

The revenue generated from external learners has to be balanced against the cost of revision and offering the service. It should also be noted that second and subsequent offerings will amortize the development costs further and contribute to the maintenance costs.

Conclusion

For an institution setting out to offer a course on the Internet, how much the institution is willing to spend to set up the course could affect the outcomes. A relatively easy generic mark-up language over a file will allow you to claim that you have a course on the Internet. In the long run, this cheap solution will lead to dissatisfaction by the learner and the material will be ignored. As such, the cost of establishing the site will not be amortized by people visiting the site or taking up the learning materials.

At the moment, an Internet site can run off a fairly powerful personal computer with modem and large disk space to handle the expected flood of enquiries and course participants. That is the minimum. More powerful personal computers and improved communications through ISDN (digital telephone lines or via ASDL or satellite) may increase the performance of your site, but the ultimate guide to performance will be the power of the equipment available to the learner and the design of the course information, which limits the courses that are available to the student.

There are costs associated with providing a service on campus and to people who have access from outside the institution, until they sign up for the course delivered on the Internet. Just as cost considerations fall into two main areas, costs for the institution and costs for the learner, benefits are available to both the institution and the learner.

This chapter looked at these costs and the benefits for:

- Institutions. Costs include:

  - capital costs;

  - cabling and connectivity costs such as software;

  - systems management.

  The benefits would include:

  - increased utilization of courses;

  - more flexible use of resources;

  - potential to generate more income from increased course enrolments.

- The costs associated with the educational considerations. This may require the following cost elements:

  - subject expert;

  - instructional designer;

  - Internet/computer person;

  - transfer and manipulation of documents;

  - copyright.

- The benefits for education include

    - the development of a quality product leading to increased enrolments;

    - the satisfaction of client needs.

- The costs for the learners include equipment costs and costs associated with the course.

- The benefits for the learner include a more effective course that they are able to access as and when they determine.

The section on budget considerations contained a description of the major items that would form part of the expenditure of developing a course for Internet delivery:

- management;

- course revision;

- maintenance costs;

- clerical;

- staff development.

It incorporated a set of schedules that might be used in the budget process.

The important point to remember is that course development and delivery arise from a need. The use of a particular technology to satisfy that need arises from an analysis of requirements. These considerations must look at the costs, benefits and the available budget alongside the educational analysis.

In the next chapter, the developing areas of the Internet will be explored.

6 Developing areas

Summary

The Internet is telephone-level technology. Because it is seen as telephone technology, there is no great mystic about the Internet. This is a very favourable situation when it is compared with the mystification surrounding the computer...with the technology jargon of CPU, mother board, input/output serial port, etc. With the Internet you look-up, log-on and you're connected. (That should be the scenario but then there is reality.)

While the Internet uses the technology of satellites and computers, the interconnection is done using currently available modems and telephone technology. The initial development of the Internet was based on text. However, there are several areas of development on the Internet and the use of the Internet as a tool for teaching and learning that move it even further away from the use of text. These are:

- audio;
- video;
- videoconferencing;
- interactivity;
- virtual reality;
- access and equity issues;
- information and research tool.

Audio

When the Internet started it was a text-based communication. The development into the World Wide Web and development tools and browsers means the Internet is capable of handling graphics, stills, illustrations, audio and animation and video. The capabilities of modems have expanded to the extent that quality FM (frequency modulated audio) is now available from many sites. This of course comes with the proviso that you have at your receiving site the modem and sound capability to take advantage of these transmitting sites.

The increase in modem capability, particularly to 56K or with ASDL to Megabyte download, increases the speed of transmission but also increases the possibility of interactive screen sharing. The speed of the lines and the error correction capabilities remove all of the frustration of screen sharing at modem speeds of lower than 9.6K. And you must remember that these modems are still in use.

It is possible with the use of proprietary brands to set up video conferencing at these higher speeds. You must remember, of course, that there are cost considerations in the move to ISDN (Integrated Services Digital Network), but this may not be a factor in the near future as telephone companies move from analogue (slow speed) to digital ISDN (high speed) technology and on to ADSL (Asymmetric Digital Subscriber Loop) and new information compression systems. In the short to near term there will be a move to higher-speed modems. This transition will support the possibility for real-time video.

Video

Video has been available on the Internet for some time. There have been problems with compatibility, leading to a degree of frustration. A particular cause is that the Internet has expanded at such a rate without a standard being established. One consequence has been the emergence of several video standards. Yet there has been a tendency for some of the options to become *de facto* standards. The position is similar to the relationship between SGML and HTML and possibly VRML. Whilst there will be an international standard (SGML), there will be working standards such as HTML. With video, MPEG (Motion Picture Evaluation Group) and TCP/IP are recognized standards (one in the United States, the other in Europe).

On a historical note, there are the audio/graphic systems combining voice and slow-scan video over standard phone lines. The next generation of video/audio standards will see the global availability of full motion video and CD standard sound available in the domestic market.

Videoconferencing

While these audio/graphic systems served a purpose and are still operating to facilitate learners learning, there is now a range of proprietary brands of interactive video systems using the new mini or finger cameras. These use software compression of the video signal and display through either a computer screen or a television screen. These systems require the same proprietary brand at the receive site to ensure compatibility. This may cause a problem if there is a failure to recognize that some parts of the world run their electrical system at a different rate. These different rates of electrical speed influence the rate at which television signals are generated and translated to images on the screen. So a signal generated in the United States is not compatible with a signal in Europe or in much of Asia. This means that these video systems have to be switched to perform at the same standard.

Some of these desktop systems are based on, or are developed from, or are scaled down from existing videoconferencing systems. In many cases, stakeholders such as technicians and systems sales people involved in the technology are critical of the slow-scan images of the 1 to 15 frames per second systems. These people want broadcast television standard. What they fail to see is the analytical possibilities that are available in slow-rate television images. These slow-rate images almost approximate to stop motion photography and therefore allow analysis of motor skills. What technologists see as a limitation, educationalists see as appropriate for education and training use in skills-based areas. The other aspect of these mini camera/finger camera systems is that they are interactive. And they are not that expensive at under A$500 for a send and receive set-up. These prices will come down and the degree of sophistication, such as multi-point sites, will increase.

Interactivity

The question of interaction in education and training is critical. Interaction is like gratification – there are three forms: instant, delayed and none. This holds for interactivity in text and audio-visual forms of the Internet.

Instant interaction is a close approximation of the classroom in that questions are raised and discussion and solutions follow. However, this quick fix disguises the very real interaction that results from the development of trust and respect that takes place in developing a collegial interaction. An impression I have when people talk about instant interaction or response is the question of speed, not the need for quality in the response. In this context, a delayed response may contain a more considered reaction to the initial request. There is a possibility in some of the applications for the Internet to create an audio-visual file and transmit that file without the need for the person at the other end to be using their computer. This has implications when messaging over time zones.

The delayed response may arise from two separate actions. The first is the receivers' need to consider a response. Often in the face-to-face setting a learner will raise a question that requires consideration. The second is the time frame involved in electronic messaging. This is mainly a question of when a learner lodges a request. The teacher they want to interact with may not be available at the time the message comes in. There could be many reasons for this 'unavailability to instantly respond'. But using the Internet will not ensure a response.

However, if over a period of time there is no interaction from the teacher in an Internet setting then there are serious considerations. When a learner signs up for a course there is an implied or real contract. Not to respond to a request from a legitimate learner is in fact a breach of contract.

Virtual reality

Given the combination of video, audio, screen sharing and animation, there is the potential for on-screen virtual reality. This has several ramifications for education and training. There are the access and equity issues and educational training possibilities.

The possibility of virtual reality on the Internet raises the issue of the virtual classroom. At the outset a virtual classroom does not seem an appropriate model for presenting course material on the Internet. The main objection is that a virtual classroom carries with it the connotation of time tabling, formatted structure for the presentation of material and an expected pattern of progression through the course. This is inconsistent with the ability of the Internet to offer flexibility for the learners to demonstrate existing knowledge and skills. I consider that courses developed for and offered on the Internet must be structured but in no way should the structure resemble a classroom. Institutions seeking to set up virtual classrooms should remember that many of the learners on the Internet are people with bad memories of their days at school. For these learners access to the Internet allows them to access the material they want and often in an anonymous manner.

Placing course material on the Internet also has the implication of shifting the cost from the institution to the learner and more directly into the community. It has to be recognized that placing courses on the Internet shifts the cost of providing places in schools and universities directly into the domestic setting, the workplace or community-based facilities. The cost of the bricks and mortar is shifted from the institutions and government to the person. It is the person who must pay for the computer power, even if rented or loaned at a subsidized fee. It is the learner who will have to pay the service provider for the connect time just so they can 'learn'.

Educational possibilities of virtual reality

Virtual reality has an image of putting on the helmet or goggles, the body suit with the tactile sensors, and playing away in a virtual world. Currently there are developments of virtual reality applications for the Internet. One of these applications is the Virtual Reality Modelling Language (VRML). This application allows virtual worlds to be constructed. Alongside this are the developments in modelling applications and animation. These will offer scope for developing educational and training packages.

The virtual world on a computer screen is similar but different. In a virtual world there are many possibilities for education and training. These could fall into the classification of scenarios. The three subsets of developing a scenario are:

- modelling;
- simulation;
- manipulation.

Modelling

Modelling requires the learner to follow a set of instructions and actions to achieve a required result. It should represent as closely as possible the normal operations, activities and responsibilities the learner would be expected to carry out as a person in the position. The intention of the modelling process is to develop learners' skills for day-to-day operations. This is similar to the use of a mentor to model examples of best practice.

Simulation

Simulation takes the scenario of the day-to-day but adds in factors that might happen to the learner when they become a practitioner. In a simulation the learner should be presented with the model setting. However, the potential for things to 'go wrong' should be a factor. The main point of using a setting of 'things going wrong' is to add to their knowledge and skills, not to fail the learner. Again, the use of a mentor could enrich this learning process.

Manipulation

With the advent of virtual reality on the Internet there is now the potential for real-time manipulation of objects on the computer screen. With this potential, the learner is able to demonstrate their knowledge and skills. There is a note of warning in that some learners in a simulation or manipulation or scenario will try to force the parameters of the setting to extremes. In a computer-based setting this is not a problem as the parameters entered by the learner should cause the warning bells to start. It is also better that the testers of the system do test the system in this learning setting rather than in the real world. It might be 'fun' to enter the wrong information in a simulation to see what happens, but this irresponsibility will not be tolerated in the real world.

Virtual reality and interactivity

The potential of interactivity offered by virtual reality and the Internet is only as strong as the interactivity through the mail, telephone or any computer-based system. The reality is that the person at the other end must respond. It is now true to state that the respondent at the other end may be a 'smart' computer.

In summary, the ability of learners to enter a virtual world has huge potential in education and training.

Educational

With the ability to enter a virtual world a learner can be presented with a scenario and work through the possibilities and as a result of the learner's input arrive at a solution. This solution will probably only be a point of the learner testing out their reactions to potential real-world scenarios. The same would hold for many training settings but there is a further potential for training.

Training

The availability of a virtual reality option on the Internet has the scope for training. The use of virtual reality offers learners the option of working with real experiences or focusing on specific skills. This ability to focus on specific skills is important in a training setting. In the real world a set of skills have to be applied in a training setting and the problem for the learner may not be one area, but a compounding of small errors across a number of skill areas. In a virtual reality/simulation, it is possible to isolate skill areas and analyse errors so that they may be eliminated. This leads to the learner stepping through the process and gaining skills and confidence to complete the task accurately.

However, there needs to be considerations about aspects of access and equity, particularly if the connect times and computing power required exceed typical home and library computing power. These aspects of access and equity apply in the use of virtual reality or any consideration of technology to support teaching and learning.

Access and equity issues

The offering of any course may have access and equity issues. Traditional institution-based courses may have access and equity issues because of rigid timetables or limited offering. This is compounded when course material is offered using technology. The use of technology raises questions about the availability of the enabling technology to the general public and to disadvantaged groups. This is a real issue and needs to be addressed. Consideration needs to be made about the public availability of computer access, the linking to computer facilities in an enterprise and the options of presenting the material in other forms to meet the needs of specific groups in the community of learners seeking access to this course material.

As I have tried to indicate in this book relating to the Internet, in my opinion the matter is not as simple as that. Two aspects that complicate matters involve the users: teachers and learners.

Teachers

A teacher perspective on using the Internet is likely to include views such as:

- What's wrong with the current face-to-face teaching structure of content and organization?

- I don't have time to handle this new technology.

- Are you asking me to develop new materials for the Internet?

Each of these expressions reinforces a view of teaching as tell, show and do. Using the Internet implies that there is a change in ownership of the construct of sanctioned knowledge.

In formal education and training, subject experts construct a view of information to be the 'knowledge', and this is transmitted to the student to create new subject experts. An assumption is that these people now have the knowledge, but a question arises about their skills to deconstruct their new knowledge into elements of information that they are able to use in 'novel settings'. However, on the Internet, and with appropriate material, it is the learner who is in charge of the enquiry process.

Learners

An existing but possibly diminishing attitude from the learner perspective is: why do we have to do it (whatever it is) this way?

Given that there are minimal access and equity problems with using the Internet as a delivery tool, the information made available to learners through the Internet (or any technology) and depending on the methodology, has three outcomes:

- incorporated / assimilated into existing 'knowledge' of the learner;

- incorporated in a unique way – this may or may not be aberrant, harmful or beneficial;

- perceived as new and unrelated information to the learner – this may be used by the learner or dismissed as irrelevant.

The learner, particularly more mature learners in competency-based learning, may ask some of the following questions:

- How is learning sanctioned?
- Can learning only happen in a formal setting?
- Do I (as a learner) need to have my learning sanctioned?
- Are teachers the arbiters, could my boss be an arbiter of learning?

As a developer of materials for Internet delivery you may want to consider other views of learners with different and equally valid assumptions:

1   Does the student understand the learning environment?
2   Learners come from a variety of backgrounds and not all of them have the same repertoire for undertaking learning tasks.
3   To be a learner, the person has skills in coping with the world around them.
4   There are issues about the learners' motivation.
5   Learners have some experience of learning in a face-to-face mode.
6   Learners lack experience in managing educational and training material.

Information and research tool

While you may consider the use of the Internet for the purpose of your course delivery, there are other aspects of the use of the Internet as an information and research tool.

The Internet can provide access for learners to a range of information that is beyond your course offering but related to it. The Internet offers access to libraries and commercial catalogues. However, for learners to take full advantage of this access to information they will need to have search skills. These search skills will need to cover:

- the search facilities (engines) of the Internet;
- a focus on topics; and

- the critical skill to evaluate and include or discard information provided by the search.

The skills involved in these search processes are higher-order cognitive skills. The search facilities of the Internet take some 'getting used to' in that the organization of the search might not result in the information you thought you were seeking. At the same time, if you allow yourself to wander off your original search topic, it is possible to find a range of interesting information but no answers to your quest. Therefore, searching for specific information on the Internet requires a certain discipline if you are not to waste hours on a non-task search. If you are thinking of allowing learners to use the range of search facilities available, it might also be appropriate to include hints about developing search strategies. This information may prevent the learner becoming frustrated in working through their search. This could be included in the scenario information.

The Internet offers the possibility of electronic mail, bulletin board, electronic chat, collaboration and teamwork, and annotation.

Electronic mail

Access to the Internet should give learners access to electronic mail. This will allow them to send messages to others. There is one problem. The learners will need to know the electronic mail address before they send out messages. If you are developing a course then you will need to consider if you want your learners to be able to mail each other electronically. You will need to consider the question of privacy, because the Internet is not a secure transmission system. Therefore some learners involved in your course may have some objection to having their personal details, such as address and phone number, on a distribution list.

One means of overcoming the privacy issue is by establishing a closed user group. With this technique you effectively limit access to electronic mail to those learners in the course. This has added benefits for the development of other mechanisms to encourage interaction between learners using the Internet.

- *Bulletin board.* Bulletin boards are a means of making course information available to the learners in the class. It is also a point where learners are able to make comment on their work or the work of others. However, without sounding like a censor, submissions to the bulletin board need to be submitted through the course manager (teacher) to make sure that the submissions are appropriate.

- *Electronic chat.* Internet Relay Chat (IRC) is a form of electronic mail. The main feature is that the messages submitted are recorded sequentially so it is possible to see the development of points of view as each of the participants reacts and responds to the previous message. Again the use of a mediator (teacher) could be of benefit to reduce the potential for misunderstanding and resultant abuse (flaming) entering into the submissions.

- *Collaboration and teamwork.* The use of these messaging systems in reality leads to the potential for collaboration and teamwork. It might be the case that some learners on the Internet are isolates. However, if given the opportunity and encouragement, most Internet learners are active participants. The reality is that an Internet connection allows participation at and when the learner finds it convenient. It also encourages the learner to ask for or seek out the information, training and collaboration to satisfy their needs.

- *Annotation.* A recent development for course providers is to allow learners to 'post queries' about information in the course. The teacher is then able to read these queries in relation to the provided information and add comments. This results in a notation appearing within the course materials. The end result is that other learners coming across this information see there is an annotation and they are able to open the annotation and see the comments. If the learner is not troubled by the course material at the point of the notation, they are able to progress without opening the annotation. This seems to be a useful device for course presenters at the time of updating the course material information.

Conclusion

A word or two of warning: there is a possible dysfunction between placing course materials on the Internet and the notion of learners being able to 'surf' the Internet. As I have stated earlier in this book, I believe that to have any validity a course on the Internet requires the maintenance of the course, the verification of the students' progress and the validation against course requirements.

This conservative approach is reinforced when I examine the introduction of other technologies into an educational and training setting. Most of these 'experiments' with technology are characterized by poor documentation, inadequate replication, discredit, and finally the failure by teachers to adopt, in any large scale, the new technology. As Marilyn Ferguson wrote: 'Innovations in education have criss-crossed the sky like Roman candles, and most spluttered out quickly, leaving only the smell of disenchantment in the air' (Ferguson, *????*).

Back in 1980, W M Gordon commented on the commercial success of television with young people and contrasted this success with the lack of success of educational television with the same young people. He projected forward on to outcomes if similar strategies were to be used for satellite delivery. He wrote:

> Television has had at best a minimal impact upon the formal education of children. Commercial development has been extraordinary...children watching...and then dutifully demanding the cereals and toys they see advertised. Considering these extremely divergent success records within the same basic population, educators must look to the utilisation of the media and not the technology... If satellite technology is utilised...without any change in the structure, role, functions and subject matter...[satellite]...will have the same impact that television had – i.e., none! (Gordon, 1980: 341)

He also is aware of the dichotomy of the new technology in an old setting. He goes on to argue that:

> The very paradox of something as twenty-first century as a satellite supporting something as nineteenth century as today's...school system...strikes at the very core of educational change. Satellite technology must be a support technology for education, but it must support an educational enterprise that is fundamentally different from that which exists in today's schools. (Gordon, 1980: 341)

Gordon is pointing to the need of the enterprise to recognize the function that technology, in this case satellite, will offer. However, he is also indicating that there is a need for the institutions to modify or change. And institutions, particularly 19th-century institutions such as schools, are reluctant to change. A decade and a half later, the same proposition must be raised about the Internet and the use of the Internet by teachers.

Edgar Stones starts to unravel the problem for teachers using technology when he addresses the underlying approach to incorporating media and technology into teaching and learning:

> In recent times, solutions to pedagogical problems have very often been sought by the use of various types of technology. Enthusiasm for aids such as language laboratories, teaching machines, closed circuit TV and currently, computers, video-disks, lasers, multi-media 'presentations' have promised the pedagogical holy grail. In due course some of them have been absorbed into the teacher's armamentarium, others gather dust in stock rooms. None has brought the prophesied pedagogical millennium. Nor was there ever the slightest chance that these aids on their own could do so, since they all took as given the 'telling' view of teaching. (Stones, 1992: 9)

Another reason for the lack of use of technology in teaching and learning is to do with the access to and manipulation of information and activities in the teaching and learning context that are predominantly teacher centred. Think back to the quote from Margret Bell earlier in this book and her list of eight reasons for the failure of information technology (IT) to have an impact in schools (education and training). The list is as follows:

- no coordinated vision

- little or no evidence of what works

- information is inadequate and it's limited

- IT in learning is not always related to solutions of real problems

- senior managers are not taking a strategic management of change approach

- educators lack confidence and competence in use of IT

- insufficient or inappropriate equipment

- insufficient or inappropriate software

(Bell, 1993: 7)

So, one word of warning is that there is in the education and training community a reluctance to adopt new technologies or adapt to new technologies. I see little reason to assume that the use of the Internet will be any different.

Then there is the challenge offered by the information age as against the manufacturing age we seem to be moving beyond. Eltis proposes that 'while acknowledging the significance of strengthening links between theoretical and applied learning, we should reject the notion that students can be prepared for the complexities of living in the 2000s by being certified that they are competent in a limited range of employment-related competencies (in the 1990s)' (Eltis, 1993: 9). The transition is from learning for a job (which was the myth of the last one hundred years), to lifelong education and training. His argument is that it is the 'do-it-yourselfers' who were the ones who explored the new technologies and it is people with a spirit of exploration who are the ones to benefit from electronic access and the informing and business aspects of the Internet, and this is not just an Australian phenomenon. Whether it be an organization such as Microsoft or a backyard operator, there is education and training and commercial gain.

7 Learners and the Internet

In the previous chapters in the book I have been putting forward views on developing teaching and learning material on the Internet. It is about time some consideration was given to the learner. In this chapter, I am considering the learner as being post-compulsory school age or at least having had some experience of formal education. This should not be seen as an assumption of the educational level of the learner. For example, anecdotal reports suggest that many adult learners have a bad school experience and seek to use other means of learning, such as distance education and now the Internet, to avoid further face-to-face school-type experiences.

While the learner has been mentioned in previous chapters, this has been in terms of access and equity issues, but there are other issues that face the learner. The purpose of this chapter is to start to address these issues, from the learner's perspective, to inform the learner. The information in this chapter is based on the small but growing field of research on student responses to the use of the Internet or computer-based learning requiring computer-based communication. My concern here is with courses that extend the learners beyond mere downloading of information. There are many reports on computer-based learning. In searching for studies using the 'full potential' of computer-based communication I came across a problem. The problem with these studies is that in the main they are small scale and taking place in the unstable environment of the evolving Internet. As a consequence, the reported results of these studies are tentative, at best, and speculative, in the main. However, as it is not my intention to turn this chapter into a literature review, I will use these speculations alongside the emerging information on Small Office, Home Office (SOHO) and teleworking. In my opinion, many of the activities carried out by SOHO operatives and teleworkers are similar to the activities that a learner using the Internet will need. The new developments on the Internet are B2B Business to Business companies).

Following a brief discussion of budget considerations for learners, the chapter deals with:

- small-scale pilots;
- ability/skills you will need;
- your learning environment;
- learning and learning styles;
- your progress.

Budget considerations for learners

In my opinion, the first thing that you need to think about before you undertake any course using the Internet is your budget. For some learners the cost of using the Internet may not be an issue. These learners will be set up with equipment, financially supported at home and work. They will be living in an environment that supports learning. This support may not be the case for other learners thinking about doing a course requiring use of the Internet.

If you are thinking about taking a course to be delivered on the Internet you need to think about the cost to you.

The costs fall into four areas:

- enrolling costs;
- equipment costs;
- online costs;
- hidden costs.

Enrolling costs

Enrolling in a course is going to have a cost. These costs may include the following:

- *An enrolling fee.* This could be called an administration fee.

- *A subject fee.* This might be a charge for subject-related material within the course you are doing.

- *A library fee.* Some institutions will charge an additional fee for provision of library services.

- *Student union fee.* As a person enrolling in an institution you may be required to pay a student union fee. This fee generally contributes towards student services on campus. As an Internet student this might seem an unnecessary charge. However, you need to check out the benefits. These can range from discounts for supplies such as computer disks and paper, to discounts on movie tickets and cheap eats.

In addition, because you are doing the course on the Internet, there may be:

- *A special equipment levy.* This could be required to 'cover' the cost of equipment loaned to you during the duration of the course. You should note that there is a seemingly decreasing tendency for institutions to provide loan equipment. The reality is that you will have to provide your own.

- *Residential/workshop fees.* In some courses you will be required to attend a residential or workshop. This might require overnight accommodation. It will certainly require travel costs. If you have family you will need to think about their support for the time you are away.

Equipment costs

At the outset, the equipment that you will need as a learner using the Internet as a means of connecting with some teaching and learning is a computer with memory, and I mean serious memory (16 Mb RAM and 500+ Mb of hard disk), a modem, a printer, and perhaps even a CD-ROM as this is another option for delivering course material. But this suggested configuration is at today's date.

You must remember that the Internet is evolving. This means that in the next months and years and as course developers seek greater sophistication, the courses and delivery may require you to have more capability, capacity, or functions in the computer to receive the course materials or take part in the electronic communication. This may result in you as a learner ending up in a technology and cost dilemma. The dilemma is that the technology driving the course outstrips your ability to finance the technology you need to 'finish' the course. The problem should not arise with short courses, for example a course that has the nominal time of six months to complete. A problem may arise where the course extends beyond six months. The reality is that the technology that supported the start of the course is superseded halfway into the course and outmoded by the end of the course. If the course organizers are worth their salt (honest in their dealings with you as a learner), they will be taking these technology changes into account as they happen. But as a learner undertaking a course with a longer length, you should consider if you will be asked (forced) to upgrade equipment at your cost. I would suggest to people undertaking longer courses that you ask the course organizers not only the minimal start configuration of your computer but possible needs for upgrades as the course progresses.

This problem of the need for technology upgrades may be minimized where course organizers provide the equipment or technology. This might happen where there are 'industry standards' for part of the course requirement. This may mean that there are contractual obligations for the course organizer to supply 'standard' equipment/technology.

If you are doing a course that is 'sponsored' through your workplace, then the minimal and potential hardware and software will need to be negotiated between your sponsor and the course provider.

Online costs

Service provider

A major question you are going to have to consider as a learner is the service provider you use. The service provider and the organization offering the course will generally not be the same organization. The service provider is only your means of connection to the course provider. In other words, the service provider allows you to connect to the organization or institution providing the course. Two considerations come in here: the first is the cost of connection to your Internet provider; the second is the cost of access and connection to the course provider.

Currently in Australia, we do not have timed local calls on telephone company (telco) standard wire-based connections. This means that I can connect to my Internet service provider through the telco for the cost of a local call for as long as I like. Then there are the fees charged by the service providers after you connect to them. These charges vary. Some service providers offer a flat fee, while others do have call limits, such as five hours a month free and then a timed fee. Some service providers also charge a fee for memory storage and downloading. In other parts of the world a telco will charge on a time basis. You will need to check the fee structure of your local telco and your Internet service providers. This becomes part of your budget considerations.

Course provider

Having worked through your telco and service provider costing, you now need to consider your course provider and other costs. These include:

- What are the enrolment costs?

- What other materials do you need and what is the cost of these materials?

- Other factors that relate to online costs include the ability to download course material and information.

In some courses the ability to download material and work offline is a considerable budget consideration. At the very least, this is a saving on online costs through your service provider.

If they are offered, you should also consider the provision of course material through other media such as print or even CD-ROM. This is not a factor of your service provider because it is a consequence of the course provider's course design and their view of course delivery. One factor in this is your learning style (mentioned below).

The cost considerations you need to take into account are:

- What are the online costs? In other words, what is your telephone and service provider bill going to be at the end of the month?

- What are your service provider costs? In reality, these are the costs for you to remain 'connected' to your service provider so that in the electronic educational environment you remain an enrolled learner.

- What are the 'upfront' course costs? These are the costs you will need to pay to be considered as enrolled in the course. These costs should cover you through to graduation or recognition for your studies, assuming you are successful. However, at the time of enrolling, ask about any ongoing fees.

And in addition to these, there are the hidden costs.

Hidden costs

The biggest hidden cost in doing any course outside mainstream delivery is the personal cost. This cost can be dramatic but in reality it is one of time, frustration and confusion.

Doing any course involves a commitment of time. Doing a course via the Internet can be more time consuming than a correspondence course. Doing a course on the Internet in the next few years could well be frustrating because the course designers have not 'got it worked out...yet'. This will lead to confusion and a cost to your health. My advice is that you should make sure that the course you are seeking to use on the Internet is robust and is supported.

Credibility of the course provider

As a learner, you need to think seriously about the credibility of the organization providing the course. You, as an 'adult' learner, are making decisions about committing time and that means expenses towards a course. On the assumption that you successfully complete the course, what credibility will your new qualification have? For example, a hidden cost could be that you have taken part in a course that does not have credibility. It is my advice that you check out the acceptance of any course offering credentials before you enrol, otherwise the 'hidden cost' is the potential waste of your time and the money you spent doing a 'useless' course.

Small-scale pilots

This section is included to alert you to the fact that some courses may not carry the full sanction of the organization offering the course because the course being delivered is a trial. As a learner using the Internet, you will have to expect that many of the courses available to you have been devised by well-meaning academics. These people will be subject experts; however, they may not be designers of instruction. Some of the courses devised and offered over the Internet will be small-scale pilots. As a consumer of one of these courses you will have to determine if the course is suitable for your need. In other words, the *caveat emptor* of 'let the buyer beware' applies. The bottom line is: their failing in instructional design should not lead to your failure.

There is another bottom line if you are taking part in a teaching and learning experiment. If you are aware of this experiment, then you should provide feedback on everything to the course delivery organizers. This will include how you came across the information on the course, the ease (or otherwise) of logging into the course, comments on course contents, activities and the learning strategies used, interactive aspects of the presentation and the results for you. You should remember that the outcomes for you may differ from the intention of the people developing the course presentation. In my experience, most course developers welcome feedback on their offering and you should offer this information.

There is a further consideration for you as a learner: you must consider your place in participating in any trial, either small or large. In my opinion, if you knowingly participate in a trial then you should expect to be supported if the trial fails. Obviously, if the trial is a success, an expectation is that no support is needed. However, two issues emerge. The first is that the trial participants need to be told of the outcomes for them and the results of the trial. Secondly, there is an underlying concern about the trial if the methodology is a success but the outcomes are flawed. This could result in you (the learner) being awarded with a satisfactory result but faulty education and training. The outcome of such education and training is that with the best will and intention in the world, you end up with job skills that are faulty.

Ability/skills you will need

Trying to work through a course that is being presented via the Internet or has an Internet component will mean different things to different people. The reason for this is that different people have different competencies with computers and differing levels of confidence. In part this has to do with learning styles and reflects on people's comfort zones.

In reality it means that you as the learner need to take every opportunity to become familiar with using the Internet.

I consider that a generic set of skills for a learner using the Internet would include the following:

- *Search skills involving thesaurus skills.* Using the Internet to find courses and information to support your learning is a bit like trying to trace the holes in a block of Swiss cheese. You find them but then... My advice is to think about your topics, define them down to two keywords, and take them as your point of departure. As my son once said: 'Using a dictionary would be easy if it had an index.'

- *'Bookmarking' or creating 'links'.* The ability to cross-reference requires you as a learner to think through possible links. You must keep in the back of your mind that the information you are seeking on the Internet has been put there by people who probably have different intents to you.

- *Downloading.* Working in the Internet environment for educational purposes really means that you need to be able to download information. This can be time consuming and, as a consequence, a cost. This also relates to the next two points.

- *Offline preparation of submissions or responses to course material.* When a course offers offline development of course requirements, this is going to be a cost saving to you. Do not assume that you will be able to work offline all the time. Some courses have real-time chat requirements. Sometimes you will have to go online to search for information.

- *Virus protection.* When you are downloading course information there is a real possibility that you may also download a virus. You should keep the highest level of virus protection you can afford. Also be careful of messages or information sent with an attachment. A file sent to you as an attachment may be infected. Not only will you inherit the virus but the potential is there for you to send the file on and infect others.

Also note that some computer sites have 'firewalls' that prohibit attachments (see An A–Z of the Internet).

Your learning environment

Learning at home

There is a historic reality or truism that teaching and learning at home takes place on the kitchen table. However, in the information age the teaching and learning is at the computer terminal. A real question is: where is the terminal situated? For example:

- Is it situated far enough away from other household business?

- Who else has proprietary rights to the computer?

- What about the phone line? Because the computer has a modem, what about incoming calls that are 'unanswered' because the modem is 'online'? Will this cause stress in the household?

- Or is your terminal at work?

Learning at work: social issues

There is an assumption that using the Internet as a learning tool to learn at work is a many-edged sword. Sanctioned learning at work means you are undertaking professional development. When this professional development happens at the workplace, several scenarios dealing with your motives emerge. You are seen as being on the promotion trail, currying favour with the boss, a go-getter or looking for another job. While managers will encourage at-work learning, you may face suspicious minds as to your motives. In the best of all worlds your desire to have further education and training will be encouraged as a contribution to the aims of the workplace.

Learning at work: practical issues

If you are learning at work I assume this learning is sanctioned by your manager and the organization. It may be that you are doing the Internet-based course in your own time or in 'company' time. The reality is that it does not matter about whose time you are using. What does matter is that you get the time to access the Internet and that your working with the course material be minimally interrupted. Minimizing interruption at work is a tricky business, particularly as you have to balance your professional development with responding to colleague and client requests so that you maintain your client and workplace relationships.

Learning and learning styles

In the area of teaching and learning there is a simplistic notion that all you have to do is tell a person something (a fact) and they will then know that thing (fact). This is called rote learning. This may be fine for new learners. But learning is also a process of adding to the old with information or skills that are new. New information is related to current information held by the learner. This form of learning, and as a consequence teaching, is far more complex. The development and delivery for this process of instruction must take into account your current abilities. This is a problem for course developers and delivery.

Your learning style

As a learner you must consider if using the Internet is the most appropriate learning device for you. Initially you must consider if using a computer is the way for you to learn. Some people find computers a threat, others enjoy the anonymity that computer-based learning seems to provide.

If you take on the challenge offered by Internet learning sites, you will need to be aware of your learning style. This includes examining if you are more comfortable learning in a face-to-face setting, from texts or in a screen-based/computer environment.

Many questions arise:

- Are you computer literate?

  Many people work with computers on a day-to-day basis. Their main tasks are word processing and the use of spreadsheets. Ask these same people about file transfer and downloading and a different (lower) level of confidence is shown.

- Do you know how to download files?

- Do you know how to 'unstuff' or 'unzip' files?

  These questions are not here to threaten; you need to know from your technology experts at the time, because the technology is evolving. In the future, there will be *no* need to 'stuff' or 'zip' files.

- How user-friendly is the institution presenting the course?

In my opinion, some institutions are placing courses on the Internet as a public relations exercise. In other words, these courses are for show. The institution is projecting an image to the public. In some cases, these course offerings will have little support for the learner. As a learner, you will need to assure yourself that the course is going to be supported.

- Do you prefer working with and talking to people?

  There is a very large temptation for people seeking to upgrade or develop their qualifications to assume that using an Internet-based course is an easy way out. The options of home and work-based learning seem enticing. In reality these may result in conflict with your personal style of face-to-face discussion and developing a network of personal contacts. The Internet does allow person-to-person contact; however, if you take the offer of an Internet-based course you may end up feeling isolated because your main contact is through a computer.

- When can you spend time to learn?

  Because you are an independent learner, any time you use is going to be a cost to you. There are arguments that you are investing in your future. (This is based on the assumption that the successful completion of the course will get you a job or promotion. However, that denies study for personal, rather than professional/employment development.) If the course is part of work, do you have any after-hours considerations such as call on time that you would normally be at home?

Your progress

Working through a course delivered by computer has a range of experiences and some of these will be frustrating. One of the biggest frustrations you may face is the time it takes for you to receive a reaction, or response, to your submission of work for marking.

In the world of electronic education and training the response time to react to a request that you send in electronically is a human factor. Currently, most of the computer systems used to support education and training are not smart enough to answer your enquiry on anything other than enrolment enquiries. What is difficult for many learners to under-stand is that the people on the other end of the line do not respond instantly. For example, you have just spent three hours compiling your submission on a course topic. You submit it to the course organizer and nothing happens...no instant feedback...no comments. As a learner, you must remember that the people you are dealing with are people. The computer will pass on your essay/information, etc, but some people do sleep at 3.00 am so you might be being a little unrealistic to expect an instant answer at that time of the morning. However, there are some insomniacs in the education and training world and you could be surprised.

Another of life's little tests when you are studying via computer is the ability to connect; there may be problems because the 'mainframe is DOWN' or work is being carried out at your local telephone exchange. In the first instance, you will have to accept the download times of the network supporting your learning. In other words, this may take some computer connect time. If the mainframe is DOWN, then get an early night or do a bit of the support reading, or talk to the family...now there's a novel idea!

But there is a further connection problem that many learners experience. This connection is to do with your expectations and the course provider's expectations. When you see the information about a course and think that this is the course for you, you need to do a reality check. This requires you to go into a 'let the buyer beware' mode to make sure that the course is what you require. From a different perspective, I see people who state what they want. However, after some discussion it sometimes turns out that what they thought they wanted was not what they need. So before you venture down the path of what could be costly in terms of your time and resources, check that the course you are considering will satisfy your need.

Conclusion

In this chapter I have attempted to address the issues that you as a learner might face when you start to use the Internet as a source of teaching and learning.

In my opinion, the Internet is not a panacea and as a learner you should not expect the Internet to satisfy all your educational and training needs. The Internet is a delivery mechanism, and there are skills that you as a user will need. Some of these skills are computer skills; however, if you are planning to learn using the Internet as a source of course information and materials, you will need to develop other skills such as search skills. Then as the Internet develops, you will need to take a realistic look at how the developments impact on your quest for learning. But before you go charging into the possible new future of Internet learning, in my opinion, if you are planning to use the Internet as a tool for learning, one initial skill you will need to develop is the skill of budgeting.

Afterword: the Internet as an intranet

In the previous chapters I have dealt with educational organizations and learners. There is, however, another area of learning and training, namely within organizations.

Intranet and organizational networking

An intranet is a network for internal communications within an organization. It has the characteristics of e-mail, file sharing and general local area network (LAN) possibilities. The main distinction is that all the communications happen in the environment of the enterprise, not just a LAN; LAN communications are generally considered to happen in a building, or on one part of a floor in a building. An intranet is more like a wide area network (WAN) but with the possibility of access to the Internet.

I use the term 'possibility' because an organization might consider that internal information should be isolated from the outside world and install an intranet with a 'firewall' to stop external access. There is another possibility. The firewall denies access, but the ancient device of a 'portcullis' at the entrance to a castle allowed interchange. The portcullis was a grate or filter. It seems to me that on many intranet sites the use of a portcullis allowing some exchange of information could be a useful design consideration.

The learning organization

There is a growing recognition that for an enterprise to prosper it must continue to learn. This is one of the driving forces behind the need for quality assurance methodologies in organizations.

Within the framework of a learning organization, the use of an intranet will facilitate workplace learning, the support of action learning teams and quality assurance. An intranet, like any network, supplies information to all members of the organization. The same level of communication means that:

- occupational health and safety (OH&S) issues are made available to all;

- internal mail is possible;

- work groups are able to communicate (the effect being meetings between formal meetings), which should add to the productivity of these groups.

The intranet and education and training within an organization/enterprise/workplace

I would assume that an organization/enterprise/workplace-based intranet education and training site has to be related to the Human Resources (HR) and pay sections of the organization/enterprise/workplace.

There are several reasons for this assumption:

- *Record keeping on staff capability*. In the interest of maintaining a record of staff capabilities and these as assets to the organization/enterprise/workplace, an intranet can serve as a means of recording training, particularly workplace experience and acknowledgement by supervisors.

- *The need to record certification on staff*. When staff gain experience or qualifications through the use of the Internet, HR managers should be informed. They may need to verify the staff development activity to maintain or increase the certification of the member of staff.

- *The potential for staff pay and conditions to change as they upgrade their skills*. The above two points relate to a possible change in pay and conditions. In the current climate of competency-based training, the incentive for the learner is an increase in the pay packet. This has to be offset against an employer's perspective of productivity improvement.

The learning enterprise organization and an intranet

Within an organization using an intranet the following three options should be available:

- *What is on offer*. In an intranet setting all offerings of staff development should be made available to all staff. Without discrimination, the appropriate level of staff to attend should be made known.

- *Access to information*. The intranet site should enable all staff access to the information. Staff and management may need to negotiate appropriate training schemes.

- *Submission of responses*. On the assumption that a staff member is sanctioned to participate in the intranet-facilitated learning, one means of the learner communicating with teachers/mentors and the like must be through the intranet.

Conclusion

Five years on from the first edition of this book, and the Internet has evolved as an interactive communication system. The actual practice is not without fault, so we should be praising the positive aspects of the use of the Web as a tool for education and training. At the beginning of this book I pointed out that:

- interactivity is a critical factor in the use of the Internet;

- an understanding of the 5 T's is critical to the acceptance of Internet-based courses;

- convergence of the technologies requires intelligent material at one end and intelligible material at the other end;

- in learning to learn on the Internet, the student needs certain cognitive, attitudinal and manipulative skills.

What must be remembered is that while the evolution of the Internet technology continues, the key consideration is the appropriate use of this technology to service education and training.

An A–Z of the Internet

These entries are written with the novice in mind as you will see from the first entry under access. The entries are also an attempt to demystify jargon.

These entries were also compiled with a view to how they might help you as a course developer placing teaching and learning materials on the Internet.

Disclaimer: Creating an A–Z on any topic is asking for trouble. Creating an A–Z for the Internet is even more difficult because the Internet is a changing entity. The entries in this A–Z will be around for a while, but for how long?

A

Access

How do I get on to the Internet?

The simple answer is you need a computer with appropriate software, a modem and connection to an Internet service provider.

What type of computer do I need?

Think about your needs. What are going to be your main tasks on the computer besides working on Internet materials? If you work in an organization that has a computer network and computer network managers, talk to these people about your plans. If you discuss your requirements with them, you are doing two things:

- You are alerting them to a possible call on the network to support the delivery of course materials on the Internet. This could cause a significant increase in activity on the network. This activity could cause other users to note that the network is not responding as they expect.

- You are also alerting them to your needs for information and service as a client. Through these discussions a working relationship should be developed that benefits you and the course material and their network.

If you are working without support, and some Internet providers run with minimal support, then a starting point for accessing the Internet to put materials on the Internet is the following:

- If you are thinking of using graphics or video clips, then think again.

- If you can only afford one computer then, preferably, you should be able to partition the hard disk. This allows development space in one partition and delivery space in the other. This provides one level of security. You should also be aware that if you are developing material and delivering material on the same computer, people may not be able access the material unless you have communication applications that allow access to the delivery partition of your hard disk as a background activity. I do not recommend this as it will make both your development partition activity slow and the delivery partition slow as well.

- You actually need two computers, one for development and one for almost full-time delivery. Two years ago, I wrote that each of the computers should have 16 Mb of RAM and something like 850 Mb of hard disk as a good starting point. In 2001, I would say that four times those figures is a minimum.

- The applications you will need to develop and deliver Internet material are very difficult to nominate. Currently, Microsoft Word offers an add-on that turns Word documents into Internet 'publications'. But there are applications such as Dreamweaver that allow a more 'hands-on' approach to Web page design.

- You will also need to contact the providers of Internet services in your area, or contact your computer systems manager, to determine the access they allow in terms of preferred systems and the charges that might be payable by the users. I also expect that in the not too distant future some providers will want statements of accountability to protect them from litigation by their clients.

- This opens up another aspect of access. These are the clients or students or learners who may want to participate in your course. You will need to consider the access to computing facilities that possible learners have available to them. These learners may have access to the Internet, but do they have the applications that will allow them to access all the course material, which might include audio, graphics and video running alongside the text?

- There are also the learners who might want to access your course through the use of terminals in local libraries, drop-in centres and community centres. You will need to consider if your course materials allow access for possible learners using these facilities.

Addresses on the Internet

An Internet address consists of several components. One example is username@computer.site.au, which breaks down into:

username (your name in computer communications)
site (this might be, for example, 'com' which indicates that it is a commercial site, or 'edu' which means that it is an educational site)
au ('au' means that the site is in Australia)

Some e-mail addresses that you might be able to access through the Internet have the same components but the user name is a string of numbers before the @ symbol. It works OK but is not as user-friendly as the username, which is generally something that you can interpret.

Administration of courses

The use of the Internet to deliver courses needs to be introduced and explained to course administrators. For example, the use of the Internet may mean that students submit work and therefore teachers submit marks outside the expected timeframe. Administrative staff need to know this so that marks are recorded in learners' records without fuss.

ADSL (Asymmetric Digital Subscriber Loop © Digital Corp.)

A version of the new technology that will allow users to see movie-quality motion on their computer screen.

Attachments

Internet mail allows you to attach other files and documents to a message. You should be very careful as some of the attachments might contain a virus, and in effect you are sending on (spreading) the virus.

A way around this is to put the attachment through your virus checker and then send it on as a plain text document. This may take some time but at least you are not the source of a virus.

Attributes

Dealt with in earlier chapters of the book. Briefly, the attribute question that needs to be asked is: What are the attributes of the course that make the Internet a suitable tool for the delivery of all or part of the course?

Audience

This is really a client question: who or what are the audience for your course and what parts of the course will be suitable to present using the Internet as a means of delivery? This requires some form of check on the potential learners' ability to access and use the Internet as a delivery mechanism.

Audio

Good-quality sound is proven to contribute to learners learning. However, like video, there are a variety of delivery standards and this may mean that learners have to go through the process of downloading audio driver applications in order to hear the sound clips. This problem is being reduced as new machines are more than likely to be audio and video (AV) equipped machines capable of handling several of the common drivers.

B

Bandwidth

The size of the line (the jargon is 'pipe') connected from your computer (see also POTS). It refers to the amount of data that can be transmitted down the line that connects your computer to the outside world. This will also depend on the speed of the modem you use. Data can be transmitted at various speeds (baud rates). Broadcast television has a broad bandwidth and this is why you need either fibre optic cable, a satellite dish or an antenna to receive broadcast television. It is possible to transmit a television-like image down normal phone lines but the bandwidth is so much narrower that there are quality problems with the images. This does not mean that the images are not useful, just that they are of a lower quality.

For comparison, broadcast television bandwidths are around 1.4 Megabits (Mbit), depending on the country and system being used, while the highest bandwidth available through standard telephone lines is moving from 14 to 28 and possibly 56/64 kilobits (kbit) in the near future.

Bookmark

Places electronic tags on sites allowing you to return to those sites without re-creating your initial search to get to the site. These could be useful in assisting students to visit like-minded sites or as suggested places to go to find further and related material.

As a course developer you will have to provide the site address, but you should then suggest that students bookmark the site for easier access at a later date. You should note that using a bookmark will not make access time to the site faster if the bookmarked site is popular.

Browsers

These are applications that enable you to access the material on the Internet.

Buttons (Thumbnails)

Buttons are a navigational device. The most obvious buttons are forward/backward and quit. However, buttons should be considered as effective educational tools. Buttons could be used to link some theory to a practical simulation. They could also be used to provide supplementary information in the manner of pop-up windows.

C

Copyright

There is a real issue about importing material from other sources and presenting them as part of course material on the Internet.

In many cases, standard copyright precludes the use of material in other than its original form. You will need to seek copyright clearance if the material is to be reproduced in an electronic form on the Internet.

Course suitability

A fundamental question that any course developer must consider when the use of the Internet is proposed is: why use the Internet? The question has been raised in other places in this book, but for those that have just started here, you need to ask yourself the following questions. What is it about this course or parts of this course that make it suitable for use on the Internet? What, if any, aspects of the course or parts of the course are more suited to delivery by other methods (eg face-to-face, text, workbooks, etc)?

CUSee Me

One of many desktop video conferencing systems. Uses standard phone lines (though you may need to check on transmission speeds between different phone companies or countries with different transmission standards).

D

Diagrams, illustrations and images

The use of this 'graphic' material is often required in teaching and learning material. However, on the Internet the use of this type of material could cause problems. These may relate to the bandwidth, the browser or the speed of the modem being used.

E

E-mail (electronic mail)

One aspect of the Internet is the ability to e-mail others. For you to be able to do this you need their e-mail address and they need yours. Fortunately, when you join an Internet service you are given an address. This address is appended to all e-mail messages you send. This raises the other problem, namely that you need to know the e-mail address of people you want to contact. In the absence of an e-mail equivalent to a telephone book, this provides one of the last remaining reasons for travel to conferences. It is only at conferences that you meet like-minded people and are able to exchange e-mail addresses.

Error messages

As a user of the Internet you will get error messages, such as '401 file not found'. The reasons for error messages fall into three general categories:

1 The site is under construction and the link to the information you were seeking has not been made by the site developer. Frequently, site developers will issue a warning at the home page if the site is under construction and therefore you can expect to run into problems.

2 Sometimes you will get a message that the site could not be found. One cause is that the site is turned off or 'down' for maintenance, or there may be too many people accessing the site, etc. However, if you try to access that site a second time, it often becomes available.

3 Error messages may be generated if the capacity of your provider is reaching its limits. In other words, there are too many people accessing the network and this is causing the system to overload. In this case, many systems will warn users off rather than have the whole system 'crash' and frustrate all users.

F

File transfers

FTP (File Transfer Protocol)

This is supposed to allow you to transfer files from your computer to another computer or on to the host computer (the file sever). Some problems arise. The file you transfer will not open because you don't have an application. It is possible to get around this problem if the creator of the file has access to and uses a run-time version. This means that you end up with a standalone version of the file.

Find

Sounds very user-friendly but in most net browsers 'find' will only find a reference in the current page (or related pages) on the screen. This means that if you are in a university home page, a 'find' request will relate only to that page. It may be that the information you require is in the university but you may have to apply some lateral thinking to your enquiry.

There are search engines which are actually sites where the site managers have conjured up topic-related sites. They look smart and they may, I repeat may, have found sources of information that are useful to you or your students.

Firewalls

Firewalls are devices to stop unwanted intrusion into computer systems. Firewalls may also be designed to stop attachments to mail messages entering the system.

Forms

Briefly, the need to generate forms should be minimized by the use of evolving templates. These evolving electronic forms may bring on the age of the paperless office in educational and training administration. However, to be realistic, this will also require a change in the mindset of administrators.

Fractals

At the moment, the downloading of video and graphics (see Video and Graphics) can be very expensive in terms of connect time and computer memory. The use of fractal algorithms is economic because the algorithm only changes those features of the screen that change. For example, the aspects of a talking head that change will be the lips, any movement of the head or blinking of the eyes. If the background is static, this is ignored by the algorithm. (See RSN.)

G

Gophers

A gopher is a search mechanism that is a historical part of the Internet.

Graphics

The use of graphics on the Internet is currently a worry. This is because people are becoming used to graphics appearing on their screens from the increasingly larger hard disks and from CD-ROM material, be it games or information material such as a CD-ROM encyclopaedia. Any site on the Internet will be hard pressed at the moment to deliver complex graphics in the same time as the same graphics can be accessed from a CD-ROM. This is because the CD-ROM is connected to or part of the computer. In an Internet setting, these graphics have to be downloaded from a remote host. This problem can be reduced if graphics are downloaded in a file transfer (FTP) but then the question arises of the capacity of the user's computer to handle the data involved and process the information.

H

Help

Help functions, like all functions in computer applications, are only as smart as the people who develop them. Unfortunately, on the Internet there are many users who have already experienced the lack of help. As these sites may change over time, or by the time you read this, it is difficult to recommend sites. I do suggest that a browse though a computer specialist bookshop might turn up further suggestions, as well as a browse on the Net.

HTML (HyperText Mark-up Language)

Often called the daughter of SGML (see below), but in reality a default standard to many. The main 'problem' will be that subsequent versions will address more complex screen presentation and interaction issues and this may (will) require extensive revision of material already developed for HTML presentation.

I

Illustrations and images

See Diagrams and/or Graphics.

Instructional design

The possibility of placing teaching and learning material on the Internet opens up another means of education and training. However, the use of any medium must take account of the positive attributes of the medium to enhance learning and limit the factors of the medium that detract from learning.

Integrity of courses

The essential question here is: how are you and your organization going to assure the quality of any course or part of a course that you offer through the Internet?

Interactivity

Emulating the traditional classroom.

Intranet

An intranet is basically an Internet for the use of those within an organization. Depending on the intranet set-up, it may be possible for users to access the Internet.

Iteration

If you offer a course or modules or units of a course on the Internet, that is an iteration of the course. As a result of feedback about the course you may decide to alter parts of the course. This becomes a new version, or an iteration of the course. If this happens frequently, soon the course will be significantly different from the one that was originally sanctioned and offered.

What strategies do you have to cover the certification of evolving courses and, more importantly, the upgrading of the information and skills of the initial learners?

J

Just-in-time

One of the most appropriate uses of the Internet is to deliver educational and training material as the learner needs it, or just in time. In reality, this delivery may be just after the learner needs it. However, for you to be able to deliver just-in-time material requires planning and preparation. This planning and preparation will enable you to cope with the expected. How will you cope with the unexpected need for just-in-time education and training?

K

Knowledge

It is an expectation of any course that the learners will increase their knowledge. This can be tested through assessment tasks that determine if the knowledge is known. There is, however, a further test that may need to be applied, namely whether the knowledge can be used in other settings.

The significance is that while knowledge has a value in its own right, the ability to apply that knowledge in a variety of appropriate settings indicates that the learner has assimilated the knowledge into a working frame of reference.

L

Learning strategies

There are learning materials on the Internet. There are qualitative measures that can be applied. The focus question in most cases is: what is the requirement of the course that makes the use of the Internet a part of the learning strategies?

Links

The Internet is about links. In the beginning, the purpose of the Internet was to set up links between like-minded people seeking and sharing information. It originated in the US, although the Web came out of CERN. It was military. It was science. Then it became education and information. And now it is going commercial.

Links between people

E-mail.

Links between people and information

Random access learning.

Logo

This is not the program of Prof. Papert. In this context, a logo is a symbol that serves to identify an institution or organization. However, a logo is a graphic element of the screen page. As such, the use of a logo takes up not only screen space but also bandwidth every time it has to be transmitted. In my opinion, a logo serves a purpose at the home page and in some of the initial menu pages. A logo should take up only a small amount of space and therefore make a small call on bandwidth in any course material.

M

Menu

One of the organizational needs and a key consideration to facilitate the learner's access to the materials. The menu will form part of your home page and subsequent levels of organization of material. On all pages a menu will be part of the navigational devices developed to assist learners. Sometimes these menus will be a 'second guess' of possible movements through the teaching and learning material by the learner. On a more general level, pages of information must be presented with the standard navigation of the browser being used.

Metacognition

A fun term to deal with! Literally it means learning how to learn. In the 'old days' terms of Bloom's Taxonomy, it extends analysis and synthesis and the cognitive behaviour of the learner into the learner being articulate about their cognitive processes.

Metadata

If we are able to talk about or define information as finite entities then the concept of metadata is needed to explain the relationship between the finite elements.

N

Navigation

This is supposedly what the Internet is all about. There are, however, some possible difficulties in getting where you want in order to get information. The first of these is thinking through how someone has classified information. For example, in this book file transfer is referenced as FTP and X-change of files.

There is also the problem of remembering where you have been. It sometimes helps if you 'bookmark' a site (in Netscape); this will allow you to return to that site direct without the need to re-create your original search.

Navigation of course material has a different context. Access to a formal course on the Internet implies that the learner is on a quest. The knowledge of the learner undertaking the quest could range from totally naive to a practitioner seeking certification for knowledge and skills gained from their life experience. As a course developer, provider and possibly accreditor of learning, you may wish to have different navigation paths through the materials to expedite the learner's needs.

Non-completion

In open and flexible delivery courses it is recognized that in some courses there are learners who do not complete the course in which they have enrolled. They may complete several subjects, but then they 'disappear'. One possible explanation is that they have achieved their goal. Other explanations range from poor course materials to losing interest. By placing course material on the Internet there is a further possibility that learners may, through their curiosity, find other sources or sites that provide information. The learners are able to access this information without the context of a course. These people are undertaking lifelong learning.

O

OH&S (Occupational Health and Safety)

Learners working on material, either in real time or using downloaded material offline, are working on a computer screen. This means that all the requirements of working with computers should be known to the learners. It is not enough to assume that a person working on a computer knows the correct work habits.

There are several actions you should take to be proactive:

- Within the content of the course, remind learners that they need to take a break away from the computer.

- Include activities that are not computer based but obviously add to the development of the learners' skills and knowledge at this point in their study.

P

Parameters

What are the parameters of Internet use? There are the attributes of a course or section of a course that indicate that the use of the Internet is warranted. But then there are the clients of a course. What are their needs?

Given the prior experience of a learner in many subject areas, they may not need a full course. What are the parameters to be used within the formal course structure to determine a particular learner's need?

This opens up questions of prior learning, certification and the maintenance of standards.

POTS (plain old telephone system)

This relates to how you can effectively use the available communications technology to provide an effective infrastructure. It requires a recognition that high-tech systems are not globally available and that a selection from available technologies may call on the use of post (at the least), radio (in combination with post), and at best post, radio and telephone to help learners to learn.

POTS (version 2)

Technologists were claiming that fibre optic cable would replace the standard twisted pair of cables that form the basis of most telephone services. New and smarter computer applications mean that POTS will have a longer life span. This will reduce infrastructure cost.

Q

Quality

This is a real issue with presenting material on the Internet. How do you put in place a certification process to assure the clients and stakeholders that an Internet-delivered course has the same integrity as a course being delivered in the face-to-face mode? The issue is really one of the transition from the old paradigm of the classroom/workshop to the new paradigm of learner-centred learning.

Questions

Elsewhere in this book, the need to ask questions and assess the learner's answers is raised. If you are using the Internet there are issues of security about the questions as they are transmitted to the learner and the security of the learner's responses.

Then there are the questions themselves. How are they developed? How is the validity of the questions determined? How is the reliability of the questions determined in relation to the expected outcomes of the course?

R

Refresh

Often when you access a site the resulting screen looks 'wrong'. Text may look out of alignment and there may be random images that don't make sense. This is probably due to faults in transmission. If there is a refresh button on the browser, click on it and your screen will be refreshed. In other words, the original material will be retransmitted, this time possibly with better fidelity. You will need to inform students of this function. Some will be aware of it, but it is particularly important if there are buttons and thumbnails that learners need to see.

Registration or recognition of the course

The purpose of this book is to enable and encourage course developers to place teaching and learning materials on the Internet. Some courses could be delivered to a greater or lesser extent using the Internet as a delivery tool with only the recognition of the course provider. The status of and award from such a course would ultimately rest within the community of the Internet and the subject experts associating on the Internet.

Other courses offered to a greater or lesser extent on the Internet will have a more formal status. This requires sanctioning at two levels. The first is of the content, the second is of the means of delivery. Without a history of course delivery, using the Internet is still an exploration. However, the Internet has status. Is status a reason for placing teaching and learning materials on the Internet?

Resources

Currently, many institutions are placing information on the Internet. As a rule, this information comprises a 'designer' home page, while the bulk of material behind the home page is straight text 'dumped' into an HTML application with at best a few links between some key words. If this sounds cynical, it is not. It is the reality, because computing departments and subject areas do not have the resources, unless they use free-of-charge students who are working on projects.

RSN

Stands for Real Soon Now.

The computing industry, and the Internet as a computer-based industry, is full of promises. If you are contemplating a venture into Internet delivery then you must do it with all senses open...including the sense that your current advice might just be out of date, or overly optimistic.

S

Screen design

With browsers, there are certain default settings that in part make a lengthy discussion of screen design unnecessary. These browsers allow the display of a limited set of attributes on a screen. This will change over time. In the interim, much of what has been researched on screen design with computer-based presentation of course material applies for presenting material on the Internet.

Several observations may help:

- *Home page design*. Many organizations have an impressive home page / front page. It only takes a little exploration into these sites to see that similar design considerations are not applied to subsequent information.

- *Extensive use of graphics/illustrations*. Serious consideration needs to be applied to the use of graphics and illustrations, not to mention video. Until fractal technology and high-speed modems become the norm, the use of graphics, illustrations and particularly video will overload computer systems. In the interim, time should be spent on developing strategies to optimize the teaching and learning potential.

- *The use of organization logos*. Logos serve a purpose, but how big is a logo in face-to-face teaching and learning materials? It will probably appear on the front page, and in some training institutions it will appear as a footer (to prevent unauthorized copying); in most educational and training material handed to students there is no logo. Yet on the Internet some institutions have templated their logo on every page. The main result is to reduce the available screen size for viewing material.

Scrolling

One of the failures of computer-based education was the need for constant clicking on keys or the mouse. An initial evident failure of transfer of material to the Internet is the need to keep pressing the down arrows or to scroll down to reel through essential page-text material.

Security of material

The use of computers in any educational and training setting presents the possibility of the computer-based material being corrupted. This may be intentional or accidental. From a course delivery and learner focus, neither should occur. This requires a plan to reduce the potential for corruption of material.

SGML (Standardized General Mark-up Language)

SGML is an International Standards Organization (ISO) recognized methodology of electronically marking up documents so that they are machine readable. The advantage of this is that the same information can be made available through translation to other resources such as CD-ROM or into print technology. HTML is a version of SGML but there are implications for the use of browsers.

Spoofing

This is actually a surrogate site enabling people to access the Internet at the local level.

Student assessment responses

This is a useful topic to follow on from security. If you have students submitting material electronically for assessment, it means that they have access to part of your computer or system. Others may also have access. Computer hacking once had a connotation of prestige. A computer hacker went into a program that was not behaving as designed and hacked away at the code until it did behave. Hacking now has the connotation of vandalism and criminality. When computer systems are opened up to access, there is the potential for hacking. While there is potential to damage course materials, there is a greater danger of hackers being able to access the semi-public mail box and either with malice or as a 'prank' interfere with student submissions. As a consequence, student responses become meaningless and the confidentiality required in assessment tasks is compromised.

T

Teaching staff change of role

If teaching and learning materials are to be offered on the Internet, then in the immediate future teaching staff will need induction on their role. In the past, teachers have had to adapt to new curriculum content. With the advent of course material being offered on the Internet there is a real challenge to teachers and their role.

Teaching strategies

These are discussed in the earlier sections of the book. The main concern is that teaching and learning materials on the Internet are presented with the same integrity as materials in face-to-face teaching.

It must be recognized that material presented on the Internet will either be part of a flexible delivery process or be the content of a delivery of a course. As such, the teaching strategies will need to account for the promotion of learners' learning, the logical presentation of content and the development of appropriate assessment tasks, evaluation and reporting.

The mere presentation of the content of a course on the Internet may be meaningful to some. The creation of meaning is a result of the new information being made meaningful in relation to information already comprehended by the learner. There are teaching strategies to assist the learner assimilate new information with the old. In preparing course materials for use on the Internet, some of these strategies could be incorporated.

Templates

Templates provide a standardized computer (or paper) outline of a document for people to fill in. A template could be an enquiry form, an enrolment form, or a format for presenting teaching and learning materials on the Internet.

Thumbnails

These are 'miniature' versions of an image or a video clip that alert the learner to more information available to them. In the past, the learner would need to have the appropriate software to allow these thumbnails to be expanded. It is more frequent that the thumbnails can be expanded because course developers are using run-time versions of the software that creates the thumbnails. (NB: A run-time version means that you do not require a registered version of the appropriate software on your computer; however, your computer may need a certain memory capacity to allow the run-time version to operate.)

As part of the screen design, thumbnails can also be used to alert the online system that a learner may want to view the contents of the thumbnail. This means that the image can be being downloaded as a background activity, in preparation for viewing, while the learner is reading the screen and making up their mind if they want to see the contents of the thumbnail.

U

Units and modules

Many courses are broken up into units and modules for the convenience of running the course. If a course runs over several years then an administration difficulty arises in judging the progress of a learner. If you break the course into units and modules that are of a shorter duration than the course, then the progress of the learner can be judged in that shorter term. This also creates a terminology problem. When you offer a course, that is, the whole entity, do you then need to offer parts that are units that have modules or do you offer modules that are composed of units? In reality, this decision may have already been made for you through the requirements of national curricula or the need to fit in with the criteria of accrediting authorities. If that is the case, the main suggestion here is to get the terminology right and be consistent.

V

Video

Video is an RSN on the Internet. The algorithms that are being developed through fractal technology are contributing to the compression of video signal bandwidth (see Bandwidth, CUSee Me and VRML).

Virtual Reality Modelling Language (VRML)

This is a field that offers huge potential for education and training. Here I cover it in terms of philosophy, education and training.

Philosophy
The ability of students to enter a virtual world has huge potential in education and training.

Education
With the ability to enter a virtual world, a learner can be presented with a scenario and work through the possibilities and as a result of the learner's input arrive at a solution. This solution will probably only be a point of the learner testing out reactions to potential real-world scenarios. The same would hold for many training settings but there is a further potential for training.

Training
The availability of a virtual reality option on the Internet has the scope for real education and training. There need to be considerations about aspects of access and equity, particularly if the connect times and computing power required exceed typical home and library computing power.

W

WAN

WAN is an acronym for wide area network. In reality, it is a bigger version of the LAN (local area network) that many of us endure. In practice, it allows a course provider to offer the delivery option to a global audience. Two criteria are required as a minimum: real site protection and actual support of students who undertake the course.

WAP

An acronym for Wireless Application Protocol. In reality, it is a bit of technology that allows you to 'communicate' between two computer devices without the need for a physical, ie wired, connection.

Work

This book and the ideas in it are about learners working with learning material. In essence, this comes down to working online or working offline.

Work 'online'
This requires the learners to access the computer containing the material they want to work with. These could be learners on campus (at drop-in centres or libraries) or off campus (at study centres or at home or work). They access the material and work with it in real time. On campus and at study centres, the overheads may be minimal because of the use of local area networks. The cost of working online off campus may become very expensive due to the time that the learner requires to be online.

Work 'offline'
This also requires the learner to access the computer and set up an online session. However, they then download (transfer) the teaching and learning materials or information they require on to their computer and conclude the online session. This process can be very short and therefore relatively cheap. Assuming that all has gone well in the downloading process, the learner is now able to work with the material. There is no cost of transfer of information back to the host (your) computer.

The learner works on the material, and will probably work on other jobs on their computer. When the learner has finished working with the material, which could be days later, they reconnect with your computer (go 'online') and submit the outcomes of their work on the teaching and learning material.

X

X-change of files

A means of quickly transferring information from your site to the user. These files can be embedded in parts of your home page and accessed only under certain conditions, such as that they are registered as learners with your organization.

The use of File Transfer Protocol (FTP) requires you to give access to your computer to the user, or to send the files to the user on request. This means that the learner and your site must be equipped to transfer files. If you are on the Internet you will have the modems but the learner may ~ed to install an FTP.

~here are security implications in both methods. In the main, if people ~e receiving and then re-sending the files back with answers to questions and assessment tasks, this resubmitted material must be sent to somewhere on your site other than the location of the original material. In other words, you should set up a receiving 'postbox' to accept this incoming material. This will in part provide some protection and integrity to your original teaching and learning materials.

XML (Extensible Mark-up Language, © IBM)

A product that allows you to add tags to information.

XTML

This is a further but not too frequently used extension of HTML. The purpose was to tag information so that it could be presented in both print and screen-based formats.

Y

Yack and chat

News groups and educational sites generally have established a part of their site where you can join in a shared screen to exchange views. This might require some experience of 'netiquette'. On some of the sites these yack places are called cafés. This is to distinguish them from tutorial or library areas of the site where more formal exchanges take place. On some sites, unless you are a registered learner you may not have access to these areas of the site.

Z

Zip file compression

Zip file compression is just one means of condensing files. An application called Stuff-it is another. Using file compression may save transmission time but the people at the other end can spend a lot of time working with the file to decompress it, particularly if they don't have the application you used to compress the file. They may have to search the Net for the particular compression you used. This can be a frustrating and annoying exercise.

References and further reading

Anderson, Tony (1988) *Trial of Course Delivery by Satellite*, TAFE, New South Wales.

Arger, G *et al* (1989) UNE/TELECOM trial of interactive video using data compression techniques, *UNE*, October.

Arnall, Gail (1988) Satellite delivery learning, *Training and Development Journal*, June.

Bell, Margret (1993) IT in learning, *The Computer Bulletin*, April.
In my opinion, this article sets out the strengths and weaknesses of the use of computers in education and training. These are also the potential underlying strengths and weaknesses of the use of the Internet for education and training.

Bloom, Benjamin *et al* (1956) *Taxonomy of Educational Objectives*, Vol 1, Longman, London.

Bloom, Benjamin *et al* (1992) *Changing Patterns of Teaching and Learning*, National Board of Employment, Education and Training, November.

Bruner, J (1990) *Acts of Meaning*, Harvard University Press, Cambridge/Boston MA.
How do we create meaning? There are physiological, cognitive, environmental aspects to how we create meaning...or is it construct meaning? A readable text that recognizes the learning ability of the newborn as a starting point for lifelong learning.

Chung, Jaesam (1991) Televised teaching effectiveness: two case studies, *Educational Technology*, January.

Collins, Valerie and Murphy, Peter (1987) A new adult student: learning by interactive satellite, *Continuing Higher Educational Review*, Spring.

Daniel, J S *et al* (1977) *The Use of Satellite Delivery Systems in Canada*, Department of Communications, Ottawa.

Davies, Ivor (1981) *Instructional Techniques*, Mcgraw-Hill, New York.
This is a useful text on the role of instructional design and technology. In my version of the book the Internet is not mentioned because it wasn't developed. The good thing about this book is that Davies argues for the appropriate use of technology and this is useful in supporting the development of materials that will support an Internet delivery or prove to be more appropriate and economical than Internet delivery.

Debling, Graham (1989) Chapter Seven in Burke, John (ed), *Competency Based Education*, Falmer Press, London.

Duffy, Thomas H and Jonassen, David (1991) Constructivism, *Educational Technology*, May.

Elliston Project (1980) *A Trial in Distance Education*, Education Technology Centre, South Australian Department of Education.

Eltis, Ken (1993) 'Reworking the post compulsory curriculum: balancing new needs', *ACE NSW Chapter Monograph*, Australian College of Education (ACE), June.

Ferguson, Marilyn *The Aquarian Conspiracy*, quoted in Bell, Chris (1988) Practising education with the new technologies, in *Education for the New Technologies*, ed Duncan Harris, Kogan Page, London.

Flavell, John, Miller, Patricia and Miller, Scott (1977) *Cognitive Development*, Prentice Hall, Englewood Cliffs, NJ.

Forsyth, Ian (1987) Seduction by satellite or never mind the content: marvel at the technology, Unpublished paper.

Forsyth, Ian (1989) Training course development advice: an application of a computer database, in *Conference Proceedings Artificial Intelligence in Industry and Government*, ed E Balagurusamy, Macmillan, Basingstoke.

Forsyth, Ian (1994) Educational imperatives for technology, *Conference Proceedings of the Eleventh International Conference on Technology and Education 1994*, eds Michael Thomas, Thomas Secrest and Nolan Estes, University of Texas at Austin.

Forsyth, Ian (1995) Teaching and learning materials on the Internet – another technology for teachers to cope with: another abstraction for learners to conquer, *ASCILITE 95 Conference Proceedings*, Melbourne.

Forsyth, I, Jollife, A and Stevens, D (1999) *Planning, Development, Delivery* and *Evaluation of a Course*, (four titles) Kogan Page, London.
This series of four books were planned to give people entering education and training a working set of guidelines and tools to assist them in working with curriculum documents.

Freire, Paulo (1976) *Education: The Practice of Freedom*, Writers and Readers Publishing, London.

Gagné, R M and Briggs, L J (1974) *Principles of Instructional Design*, Holt Rinehart and Winston, New York.

Gordon, W M (1980) Communications satellites and the future of elementary education, *Unicorn*, **6** (3).

Gordon, W M (1980) in *Unicorn*, **6** (3), from Communication satellites and the future of elementary education, *World Future Society Bulletin*, **12** (3), May–June, p 13.

Gough, J *et al* (1981) Policy issues in planning for distance education using domestic communication satellite, *Distance Education*, **2** (1).

Havelock, R G (1971) *Planning for Innovation through Dissemination...*, Centre for Research and Utilization of Knowledge, Ann Arbor, Michigan.

Hayes, Kathleen and Swisher, Robert (1992) Student and faculty attitude towards compressed video instruction, *Educational Technology*.

Hill *et al.* (1991) *It Just Doesn't Happen*, Ministry of Education and Training, Victoria, April.

Holmberg, B (1977) *Distance Education: A survey and bibliography*, Kogan Page, London.

Hughes, Peter (1990) Ol' Dick Tracey might get us yet, *Sydney Morning Herald*, Sydney, 9 February, p 3.

Kitt, J *et al.* (1983) *School of the Air*, Queensland Department of Education.

Knowles, Malcolm (1984) *The Adult Learner: A Neglected Species*, Gulf Publishing, Houston, TX.

Krathwohl, David R *et al* (1964) *Taxonomy of Educational Objectives*, Vol 2, Longman, London.

Kuhn, Thomas (1970) *The Structure of Scientific Revolutions*, University of Chicago Press, Chicago.

Laurillard, Diana (1987) Computers and the emancipation of students: giving control to the learner, *Instructional Science*, **16**.

Laurillard, Diana (1993) *Rethinking University Teaching*, Routledge, London.
In this book, Laurillard sets out a new paradigm for teaching in a university setting. In my opinion, most of her arguments apply to post-secondary and lifelong learning.

Lohr, Steve (1993) Plans for grand marriage of office equipment, *Straits Times* [NYT], 12 June, p 7.

Marsh, Colin J (1986) *Curriculum*, Ian Novak, Sydney.

Marsh, Colin J (1993) Microsoft, 2 cable giants to create 'cable TV' software, *Straits Times* [NYT and Reuters], 14 June, p 7.

Merrill, M David (1991) An introduction to instructional transaction, *Educational Technology*, **31** (6).

Merrill, M David (1993) Instructional transaction, *ASCILITE 93 Conference Proceedings*, Southern Cross University, Lismore.

Moorcroft, Bob *et al* (1987) *Potential Use of 'SKYCHANNEL'*, New South Wales Department of Technical and Further Education, July.

Mory, Edna H (1992) Use of information feedback in instruction implications for future research, *Educational Technology Research and Development*, **40** (3).

Muller, Dave and Funnell, Peter (1992) An exploration of the concept of quality in vocational education and training, *Educational and Training Technology International*, **29** (3), August.

Perkins, D N (1991) Technology meets constructivism, *Educational Technology*, May.

Porter, Paige *et al* (1992) Competencies for a clever country, *Unicorn*, **18** (3).

Reigluth, Charles M (1992) The imperative for sytematic change, *Educational Technology*, **32** (11).

Rheingold, Howard (1992) *Virtual Reality*, Mandarin Paperbacks, London.

Resnick, Lauren (1987) The 1987 Presidential Address: learning in school and out, *Educational Researcher*, **16**.

Rogers, Carl (1969) *Freedom to Learn*, Charles Merrill, Ohio.
  In this book Rogers sets out the concept of teachers as coordinators of learning experiences. This is important for teachers as managers of learning. However, it is important for teachers responding to learners' needs and requests. It is a prelude to the paradigm shift to teachers as mentors and the Internet as the delivery tool.
Romoszowski, A J (1981) *Designing Instructional Systems*, Kogan Page, London.
  Sets out a schema for designing instruction. Although written before the Internet came into widespread use, it contains one view of instructional design that could form a basis for instruction on the Internet.
Romoszowski, A J (1984) *Producing Instructional Systems*, Kogan Page, London.
  Sets out a schema for designing instruction. It was written before the advent of the Internet, but the instructional attributes of vision and sound are applicable to current Internet delivery options.
Romoszowski, A J (1987) *Designing Instructional Systems*, Kogan Page, London.
Sarno, Tony (1991) Soon phones will put a face on the voice, *Sydney Morning Herald*, 23 July, p 3.
Schamber, Linda (1988) Delivering systems for distance education, *ERIC Digest*, May.
Schmitt, Maribeth and Newby, Timothy (1986) Metacognition: relevance to instructional design, *Journal of Instructional Development*, **9** (4).
Spoonley, Neil (1993) Technology and education, *Computer Bulletin*, April.
Stenhouse, Lawrence (1975) *An Introduction to Curriculum Research and Development*, Heinemann Educational Books, London.
Stones, Edgar (1992) *Quality Teaching: A sample of cases*, Routledge, London.
  A concern for the constituents of quality teaching. Not directed at the Internet but at teaching.
Whiting, John (1988) New perspectives on open and distance learning for adult audiences, in *Education for the New Technologies*, ed Duncan Harris, Kogan Page, London.
Zuckernick, Arlene (1980) *Towards a Model of Satellite-based Instruction*, University of Victoria, British Columbia, Canada.

Since the first edition of this book, I have been monitoring the growth of educational and training Web sites, such as UNEVOC, IEEE, NCREL, C3, EdNA, OECD, particularly CERI, etc. This monitoring is to capture the expectations of these organizations and to reflect on them in the text of this book.

Index